REFORMED WORSHIP
WORSHIP THAT IS
ACCORDING TO SCRIPTURE

SECOND EDITION

Terry L. Johnson

Truth for Life
Series Editor
J. Ligon Duncan III, Ph.D.

 Reformed ACADEMIC PRESS

ISBN: 978-0-9800370-9-8

Reformed Academic Press
Post Office Box 5013
Jackson, MS 39296-5013

Book Design by Word Association
Cover Design by Geoff Stevens

Printed in the United States of America

ISBN: 978-0-9800370-9-8

9 780980 037098

TABLE OF CONTENTS

1. GETTING ORIENTED

NEWSPAPER ARTICLES, MAGAZINE ARTICLES, AND BOOK TITLES all tell the tale of that which nearly every congregation in America has experienced: "Worship Wars."[1] Nor has this war stopped at our shores. The same battles that divide domestic congregations between the young and old, the contemporary and the traditionalists, the white from the minority, also divide mission agencies, mission fields, and national churches around the world. The influences of the baby boom generation, mass culture, and the charismatic movement have converged to bring rapid, controversial, and popular change. The forms of traditional worship: historic orders of service, organs, hymns, metrical psalms, creeds, "pastoral" prayers, and Biblical sermons have been jettisoned in favor of the forms of contemporary culture: soft rock, talk-show format, a friendly, informal atmosphere, overhead projector, and topical sermons addressing felt needs.

Presbyterian and Reformed churches have not been left untouched by these trends or the resulting conflicts. The whole range of "styles," from "seeker-friendly" to charismatic to contemporary to liturgical counter-reaction may be found even in conservative Presbyterian denominations. If a recent observer is right, many of these developments are all but irresistible.[2]

---

[1] E.g. Michael S. Hamilton, "The Triumph of the Praise Songs: How Guitars Beat Out the Organ in the Worship Wars," *Christianity Today* (July 12, 1999), 29-32; Elmer Towns, *Putting an End to Worship Wars* (Nashville: Broadman & Holman Publishers, 1997).

[2] Emily Brink, "Trends in Christian and Reformed Worship," *Calvin Theological Journal*, 32 (1997), 395-407. She argues that Reformed worship will become more generic (borrowing especially from the charismatic movement), more diverse, more experiential and less rational, more seeker-sensitive, making more use of the laity and becoming more based on the church calendar.

In a review of a book by a Reformed theologian purporting to be a "refreshing" defense of contemporary worship, Darryl Hart asks the question: "It May Be Refreshing But Is It Reformed?"[3] The assumed, but untested, conviction among those making the changes is that the Reformed faith can be grafted into any form of worship, be it revivalistic, liturgical, charismatic, or contemporary, and still flourish. This is an interesting theory, but it is only a theory and remains unproven. Moreover, there are good reasons for skepticism. My own background encourages considerable reservation. I was reared in the revivalistic Baptist tradition and attended the Grace Community Church of John MacArthur during the mid-1970's. From both sources I developed a high view of preaching, whether expository or evangelistic. As a student at the University of Southern California I received wide, and at the time deeply appreciated, exposure to the choruses and Scripture songs coming out of *Maranatha!Music* and the Jesus Movement. From them I learned something of the power of music to move the emotions. My first two years at seminary were spent at Trinity College in Bristol, England, where through daily use of the *Book of Common Prayer* I learned the value of reverent, structured liturgy. While I appreciate these traditions, I do not believe that they provide forms that are adequate to express and perpetuate the Reformed faith. The "low" churches lack the sense of the glory and majesty of God that results from well-ordered God-centered worship. The "high" churches lack the spontaneous and personal "feel" of Reformed worship with its free prayers and

---

[3] Darryl Hart, "It May Be Refreshing But Is It Reformed?," *Calvin Theological Journal*, 32 (1997), 407ff. The book reviewed is John Frame's *Worship in Spirit and Truth: A Refreshing Study of the Principles & Practice of Biblical Worship* (Phillipsburg, New Jersey: Presbyterian & Reformed Publishers, 1996). With the publishing of his second volume on this issue, *Contemporary Worship Music: A Biblical Defense* (Phillipsburg, New Jersey: Presbyterian & Reformed Publishers, 1997), Frame has established himself as the New School theologian of our day. Consequently, we will be interacting with him regularly as we develop the historic view of Reformed worship.

expository preaching. The Biblical and experiential balance that is the Reformed faith is best expressed in the form of worship that it generated, that is, the Reformed tradition of worship. Moreover, it is doubtful that the Reformed *ethos*, that bundle of elements that make us Reformed, such as theology, world and life view, polity, piety, and worship, can be grafted onto alien forms and still survive.

It is of no small interest that Jesus finds himself in a debate about worship at the Samaritan well (John 4:7ff). There is nothing new about controversy in this realm! His seminal words on the subject will provide principles by which we attempt to address the question we face. What question? Let us try to frame it in as narrow and precise a manner as possible in order to avoid getting sidetracked. Among the myriads of issues surrounding worship that might be discussed, and among the countless approaches that one might take to those issues, I propose the following question: *What ought we to do in the public worship services of the Lord's Day?* I believe that this simple question will provide the focus which is necessary if we are to discuss the heart of the issue without being diverted by secondary debates. Addressed in this way it will allow us to make the distinctions that must be made if we are to avoid confusion. Let me explain what we don't mean by this question before we press on to what we do mean.

Opening Questions

Public versus Private

First, the question for consideration is not what might be a valid expression of worship in the privacy of one's own closet or in the context of one's own family. Some recent writers have tended to obscure the public/private distinction, if not attack it outright.[4] Yet differentiating between public and private behavior

---

[4] John Frame, *Worship*, 44ff. Frame argues that the application of the regulative principle only to formal or "official" services is "unscriptural." "The New

is a critical application of Biblical wisdom (reference: see the Book of Proverbs). For example, clothing which might be appropriate and acceptable in the privacy of one's home could be judged immodest, provocative, and seductive merely by moving the wearer to a public setting. Bodily functions which are natural and God-given may be expressed righteously in private, but public expression would be vulgar, crude, and even evil. Marital intimacies may be perfectly valid and even righteous expressions of affection in private. But take the same intimacies, and place them in a public setting, and what was righteous immediately becomes wicked and evil. In the realm of worship itself, Jesus taught that postures and expressions which might be appropriate in private prayer are inappropriate in public because they draw attention to oneself. The setting, the street corner

---

Testament simply does not make that distinction," he claims, and so "it is virtually impossible to prove that anything is divinely required specifically for official services" (*Worship*, 44). He labels this the "Puritan" view, and concludes that if the regulative principle applies at all, it must apply to all worship, public and private, formal and informal. He argues quite vigorously for this view. "I reject the limitation of the regulative principle to official worship services . . . it governs *all* worship (his emphasis), whether formal or informal . . . limiting the doctrine to official sanctioned worship robs it of its biblical force" (*Worship*, 44, 45). But as is often the case, one wonders who these Puritans are to whom Frame is referring. No Puritans, or for that matter any other mainstream spokesman for the regulative principle, would have argued that it applies only to public worship and has no application in private worship. Rather their point and ours would be that it applies *differently*. For example, one would not be free to sacrifice a goat in family worship, or burn incense, whereas one should read the Bible, sing Psalms, and pray. In these instances the application is the same, public and private. On the other hand, one may not (as the Puritans would have argued) administer the sacraments in family worship. Why? At least at one level the answer is because the regulative principle applies differently. What is permitted publically, at officially called and sanctioned services, is not permitted privately. All worship, then, is regulated by God's Word, *but the application is different in different contexts*, whether formal or informal, public or private.

versus the closet, is crucial (Matt 6:4-6). In connection with the Lord's Supper, Paul asks directly, "Do you not have houses in which to eat and drink?" (1 Cor 11:22) The eating which would have been appropriate at home was inappropriate in public. Also, there are questions which might be asked at home which should not be asked in the public assembly (1 Cor 14:35). These few examples illustrate the point that the public/private distinction is vital, and that the Bible, sometimes explicitly and sometimes implicitly, insists that we make it. It is critical in determining both ethical and liturgical norms. A thing that may be permitted in private or family worship may not be appropriate in public worship. For example, in family worship we might all show up in our pajamas. I might ask questions of my children, take their prayer requests, and allow them to determine the song selection. But such apparel and such parent/child interaction normally would be inappropriate for public worship. In a small group study, we may all discuss the passage being studied and pool our opinions as to how it is to be understood and applied. We might even sip coffee and serve cookies while doing so. This may be unoffensive and appropriate in an informal and private setting. But in public worship? Probably not. The question then is *not* what may be a valid practice in my private devotions, in family devotions, or in a small group Bible study. Our interest is in determining what activities are appropriate in the public assembly of the Lord's Day. It is mistaken to think that the Bible does not make these distinctions, and more mistaken to think that we should not and must not make them.

"Broad" versus "Narrow"

Second, the question is not what qualifies as worship in the "broad" sense as opposed to the "narrow." It may be properly pointed out that the Apostle Paul likens all of life to a worship service in which we "present" our bodies as a "living and holy sacrifice" in a "spiritual service of worship" (Rom 12:1). There is a true sense in which we may glorify God in all of life. This is true whether we "eat or drink or whatever" we do (1 Cor 10:31). This is worship in the "broad" sense. In this sense I may be said to honor or worship God whether I am digging ditches, flying kites, or bathing my children. This is all well and good. But, some recent discussion has obscured the distinction, arguing as though whatever qualifies as the former may belong in the latter.[5] Thus some argue that because God may be glorified through music, through dance, through drama, through video clips, no objection should be raised against their use in public worship. But whether or not a thing glorifies God in "all of life" does not answer the questions as to whether or not it ought to be done in public worship. We may appreciate all these activities and agree that God may be honored through them, and yet this does not prove that they should be admitted into the public assembly. Whether or not I ought to dig ditches, fly kites, or bathe my children in the context of public worship is not the same question as whether or not God may be glorified by them. It simply is not true that every God-glorifying activity and expression may therefore be moved from the broad context of all of life into the narrow context of the public assembly. The specific question which we must answer is, what ought to be done in the public worship of the Lord's Day, not what may glorify God generally.[6]

Permitted versus Proper

Third, the question is *not* merely what may be *permitted*, or even *what might one get away with and still be within the bounds of Scripture's regulative requirements*. Reformed worship may not be

---

[5] Frame, "Some Questions About the Regulative Principle," *Westminster Theological Journal*, vol. 54, (1992), 357-366. Elsewhere Frame says that there is not "a sharp distinction between what we are in the meeting and what we are outside of it . . . the difference between worship in the broader sense and worship in the narrow sense is a difference in degree" (*Worship*, p. 34).

[6] See T. David Gordon's response to Frame, "Some Answers About the Regulative Principle," *Westminster Theological Journal*, vol. 55, (1993), 321-329.

reduced to the regulative principle, particularly the regulative principle narrowly constructed, any more than the Reformed faith can be reduced to "Five Points." The regulative principle, interpreted merely as lists of approved and disapproved elements, does not address (when understood narrowly) a fundamental ingredient of worship: reverence. It does not address matters of decorum. It does not address words and actions appropriate to a reverential approach to God.[7] No, our question is what *ought* to be done in public worship. It may be permissible for a church to begin its worship with the song "Deep & Wide," then sing as its second hymn "Zaccheus Was a Wee Little Man," and conclude the service with "The B-I-B-L-E." "Scripture does not forbid it," a strict Biblicist might say.[8] But such would be of doubtful propriety. We can even say that such ought not to be done under normal circumstances. Yet we say that, not because there is a Bible verse that forbids these children's songs, but because of a more general sense of what is appropriate in light of the nature of the Sunday assembly as the church's public service of worship. Not every question in worship or life can be answered by the direct application of a Bible verse. Indeed it is legalistic and fundamentalistic to expect to do so. Right living rarely consists of simply applying the Bible's rules to circumstances. Rather, right living requires the illumination of the Holy Spirit and wisdom in applying general principles to daily choices. Pharisees limit the Bible's application to the specific words – you shall not kill,

---

[7] We are leaving aside for the time being the question of whether or not the regulative principle should be narrowly constructed. Since the regulative principle appeals to the third commandment for support, we see reverence and related matters as being contained within its framework.

[8] We have lost track of the number of times that Frame claims that some traditional practice is "unscriptural" or that "Scripture nowhere says" or there is "no scriptural reason" or "Scripture nowhere commands" that practice when in fact it is based on both scriptural examples (not just commands) or a sense of propriety regarding public worship. *Worship* xii, 44, 53, 70, 73, 82, 93, 104, 129, etc.

commit murder, and so on, and ignore the broader application. But the broader application is where most of life is lived, and it is here that Jesus criticizes the hypocrites of His day (Matt 5:21-48). Most of life is lived "between the lines" of explicit commands.

Consequently, the Apostles regularly appeal to what is "fitting" or "suitable" or "proper," in light of Scripture's explicit commands, and yet without spelling out exactly what these things mean. They expect that believers will apply wisdom and discern what is appropriate. Thus we are to judge what is *"proper"* (Gk. *prepo* = to be fitting, seemly, suitable) about hair length, even discerning such from nature (1 Cor 11:13, 14). Paul tells Titus to "speak the things which are *fitting* (Gk. *prepei*) for sound doctrine" (Titus 2:1). Women are to adorn themselves with *"proper"* (*prepei*) clothing (1 Tim 2:9, 10). Paul tells the Ephesians to avoid talk that is *"not fitting"* (*prepei*) (Eph 5:3, 4). In the last two cases some of the details are fleshed out. Women are to dress "modestly" and "discreetly." They are to avoid ostentatious display by not braiding hair or wearing gold or pearls or costly garments. "Silly talk" and "coarse jesting" are listed among the unfitting words. But in these and all other cases the precise point at which one crosses the line from modesty to immodesty, from discreet to indiscreet, from fitting to silly or vulgar, is not and cannot be spelled out. We only know the difference through Spirit-given wisdom. When is a dress too short? At some point it is, and the sin of immodesty has been committed, objectively and actually. The determining of such is a subjective judgment. Yet, the failure of subjective judgment leads to objective sin. Nearly all behavioral judgments (e.g. love, modesty, frugality, integrity) are arrived at in this way, in applying wisdom in realms beyond the direct application of specific commands.

In worship the same sort of judgments are required. We are not merely to ask what is permissible, but what is appropriate, proper, and fitting. For example, we are commanded to worship with "reverence and awe" (Heb 12:28). There are ways of singing, praying, and preaching that are irreverent. There are extraneous words and actions that, given the nature of God, the nature of the assembly, and the practical requirements of reverence, are inappropriate, improper, and unsuitable. But in any given case this may be discerned to be so, not because there is a verse that specifically says, for example, "Thou shalt not begin worship by dribbling a basketball down the center aisle" (as did one conservative Presbyterian pastor), any more than a verse may be found to specify that skirts may be 1 inch above the knee, but not 1-1/2 inches. A television preacher recently led his congregation to respond enthusiastically to a beautiful solo by saying, "And all God's children said," at which point they joined him in saying, "Wow!" No single verse forbids "wow" as a liturgical response. These sorts of things are only discerned by wisdom. The Bible expects and demands that we move beyond narrow, legalistic, fundamentalistic constructions of what is permissible in worship, and ask instead what *ought* to be done when the church assembles for worship. "All things are lawful," says the Apostle, "but not all things are profitable" (1 Cor 6:12; 10:23).

We versus They

Fourth, the question is not what *I* personally want, or what my *congregation* wants, or what my *generation* wants, or, heaven forbid, what my *faction* wants. The question is an "ought" question, and we raise it not for our group but for the *whole church together*. What ought *we* to do in public worship? For about a generation now this question has been answered idiosyncratically, with each minister or "worship team" or church or group making its own decisions without regard for the communion of the saints and unity of the broader church. This cannot continue to be acceptable for catholic and connectional denominations. There is, after all, only one baptism, not many (Eph 4:4ff). When baptisms or other forms of worship are multiplied, it becomes virtually impossible for the church to remain unified. If the church is not unified in worship it is not unified in any meaningful sense at all, whatever claims to the contrary might be made. The questions of unity and diversity are old and complex; but we cannot help but conclude that, in our day, unity has been compromised at the expense of diversity. There is no longer an identifiable worship amongst conservative Presbyterian and Reformed churches. As we have already noted, some congregations have moved in a high liturgical direction, some have moved in a contemporary "seeker-sensitive" direction, and the others lie all along the spectrum between the extremes. This development is unprecedented in the history of Reformed practice, an experiment driven no doubt by noble ends, such as outreach and evangelism, but an experiment nonetheless, the final results of which have not received serious attention. For example, how will conservative Presbyterian denominations hang onto their members as those members relocate to new communities if they find themselves in sister congregations that look nothing like those they just left? We have pointed to the considerable anecdotal evidence already available of this happening along the traditional/contemporary divide. Those who think that loyalty to the "Five Points" and the doctrine of inerrancy will hold the denomination together underestimate the emotive power of familiar forms.[9]

Consequently we ask the question: how will the conservative Presbyterian denominations keep from fragmenting into a thousand different factions if today's liturgical multi-culturalism is not restrained? The current "best thoughts" on missiology insist on ministry forms distinctive to the tastes and preferences of each subculture at home and abroad.[10] Such ministry includes the church's public worship. So then, the young must have their worship and the old theirs. Similarly, "contemporary" whites, Hispanics, African-Americans, Asians, and, presumably, the

---

[9] See Terry Johnson, *Leading in Worship*, (Oak Ridge, Tenn: The Covenant Foundation, 1996), 2.

[10] Frame argues that music must be "meaningful" to the worshiper which he identifies with intelligibility, which he says "implies contemporaneity." Thus does my preferred form of popular music become the music of public worship and the church begins its journey down the road of liturgical Trotskyism. John M. Frame, *Contemporary Worship Music*, (Phillipsburg, NJ: P&R Publishing, 1997), 17-20.

Rednecks, the Skateboarders, and the Surfers, etc. Behind this thinking is the insistence that all music, language, and format are created equal, an aesthetic relativism, if you please. Yelps of elitism accompany any call to propriety, aesthetic standards, the Reformed tradition, or catholicity. *A more perfect philosophy for dividing and separating the church into affinity groups can hardly be imagined.* One recent author refers to the "hall of mirrors" question raised by generationally specific ministry. "When will it ever stop?" he asks. "The potentially endless proliferation of new subgroups begins to look like it is based on nothing more substantial than catering to new styles."[11] However, we are convinced that a consensus must be reached and a significant degree of uniformity must be achieved if the church is to transcend the cultural differences that Christ commands her to transcend (Eph 4:4ff; Gal 3:28; John 17:27ff). Church-wide, even denomination-wide, uniformity is not an optional goal. Catholicity of practice is an apostolic expectation and demand. Dealing directly with the subjects of prayer, the role of women and the Lord's Supper the Apostle Paul says,

> . . . *we have no other practice, nor have the churches of God* (1 Cor 11:16)

The Apostle assumes the positive value of uniform practice and demands that the church at Corinth conform to it. What the "churches of God" practice they must practice.

A second time in that same epistle the Apostle Paul lays down requirements (i.e. regulates) concerning prayer, singing, prophesying (preaching), the role of women, decency, orderliness, and underscores his authority by an appeal to catholicity:

> *For God is not a God of confusion but of peace, as in all the churches of the saints* (1 Cor 14:33; cf. 1 Cor 1:2; 4:17)

Furthermore, we are convinced that consensus and unity can only be accomplished through abandoning the current novel

---

[11] Dieter & Valerie Zander, "The Evolution of Gen X- Ministry," *Regeneration Quarterly*, 5.3, (1999), 17.

theory of cultural and generational accommodation, and aiming instead at worship that transcends narrow cultural interest and appeals broadly on the basis of Biblical standards and universal aesthetic qualities. This was the ideal to which previous generations aspired. The *Genevan Psalter*, for example, was quickly translated into Dutch, German, English, and Spanish (and a half-dozen other languages including Italian, Bohemian, Polish, Latin, and Hebrew),[12] along with adaptations of Calvin's *Form of Church Prayers*. Similarly, previous generations of Presbyterian and Reformed missionaries took their Orders of Service and Psalters into foreign lands because these were perceived not as the expression of a particular culture, but rather of an ecclesiastical culture that was catholic and transcendent.[13] Unity, not diversity, is the ideal. It is the *best*, not one's *bias*, that provides the foundation for this transcendent and universal church culture.[14]

---

[12] John D. Witvliet, "The Spirituality of the Psalter: Metrical Psalms in Liturgy and Life in Calvin's Geneva," *Calvin Theological Journal*, 32 (1997), 273.

[13] Calvin, for one, was insistent that the church's music be its own. He opposed the use of secular tunes and urged that tunes be characterized by gravity and majesty. See Witvliet, *Ibid*, 273-297.

[14] Frame's discussion is in the opposite direction and we think untenable, if not a classic case of *reductio ad absurdum*. While he concedes that "questions of quality and appropriateness" must be considered, his real concern is that no individual's or group's tastes or preferences should be imposed on any other. Consequently, "everyone's music should be heard" (*Contemporary*, 25). For Frame the whole question is *my* taste versus *your* taste, and since no set of preferences can be regarded as superior to any other, then all must have equal representation. In case you missed the point, he even gives examples of what he means by "everyone's music": "old people's and young people's music; European, African-American, and other ethnic music; complex music and simple music." For us, the whole discussion is off base. 1. It is *misleading*. The music of the church is not the music of any group. It is misleading to speak of "old people's" music – the World War II generation did not bring its cultural preferences, Tommy Dorsey and Benny Goodman for example, into the sanctuary. The church has had its own language and music which transcends the tastes and preferences of any particular group or generation. The baby boomers are perhaps the first generation in the history of the church to attempt to impose its musical preferences on the

"The church is the place where generational differences are to be transcended, not reinforced," says Gene Edward Veith. "Only a church which resists being merely of one generation can be relevant to them all."[15]

Evangelism versus Worship

Fifth, the question we wish to answer is what ought we do in a *worship* service, not what may we do in other settings on other

---

rest, and claim that only then can worship be "meaningful" to them. This comes close to generational blackmail. 2. It is *naive*. He attributes the conflict over music and worship style to "selfishness," but not on the part of the revisionists. No, he has in mind the traditionalists who are reluctant to bow to their ultimatum. An unwillingness to do so is condemned as selfish insistence on "individual preferences" over "scriptural standards." This is a remarkable exhortation given his role in urging the church down this road of catering to individual and group preferences. Those trying to protect historic Reformed worship with its simple, spiritual, and substantial forms, its time-proven quality and worth, its genius for expository preaching, free prayers, great hymns and metrical Psalms are lectured – "we must be willing to consider others ahead of ourselves" (*Worship*, 84). That there may be more to the resistance of traditionalists than taste seems not to have occurred to him. Traditionalists are defending principles, not preferences. 3. It is *unworkable*. This worship smorgasbord of cultural expression in language and song is impractical. How is each group to be served in any given service? Shall we have a liturgical quota system? What would such a service look like? Then, what if our group is under-represented in the song selection? Shall we protest? Or more likely, shall we start our own church to cater to our own tastes? Or, perhaps just a separate service. This familiar scenario of generational and ethnic segregation underscores our conviction that Frame and others have ventured down the wrong road. Personal tastes and preferences should not have been introduced into the discussion of worship. The church should transcend, not mimic, contemporary pop culture.

[15] Gene Edward Veith, "Through Generations," *For the Life of the World*, (March 1998), vol. 2, no. 1, 9. Veith also says, "When we are singing hymns in church, we are not following the preferred 'style' of anyone in the congregation. This is church music, wholly different, whatever its origins, from the currently preferred musical taste of any of the generations assembled to worship. No one is offended; no one is excluded; everyone is lifted out of a particular time, generation or in-group, into the extra-ordinary experience of worship."

days. We understand the purpose of worship services to be worship. Obvious, you say? Not to everyone. A landmark event in my own worship pilgrimage occurred while walking to chapel one morning about six months into my first year as a student at Trinity College in Bristol, England. I had endured the first six months of daily Prayer Book chapel services gritting my teeth, finding the experience almost intolerable. (When told that only 3-6% of England was in church on any given Sunday, I thought, "well, no wonder.") To me it was confusing, medieval, foreign, and worst of all, boring. But that one morning a new thought entered my mind — *the reason why you go to church is to worship God.* That thought was altogether novel for me, stimulated primarily by the God-centeredness of the Prayer Book service. I was accustomed to congregation-centered services: worship as revival service, as Bible lecture, as fellowship ("Body Life"), and as song service. More than anything else, it was the God-centeredness of the Anglican service that had been foreign and boring to me. What I needed was to understand worship from a new perspective, one which took me out of the center and replaced it with the praise of God.

Congregations sometimes assemble for other purposes, such as to hold evangelical meetings, Bible conferences, conduct church business, or enjoy fellowship meals together. But during the time designated for worship the church should limit itself to those activities that can legitimately be considered devotional exercises. The integrity of the worship service, as a service of worship, should not be undermined by otherwise worthy ends such as fellowship, church business, evangelism, Bible instruction, or anything else. Some of these are secondary ends of worship, others are byproducts of true worship. As we worship, we enjoy the exposition of the Word and the fellowship of the saints. Evangelism takes place during worship as a result of Christ-centered Biblical exposition, as well as through the net impact that a worship service makes. The unbeliever,

> *is convicted by all, he is called to account by all, the secrets of his heart are disclosed; and so he will fall on his face and worship God, declaring that God is certainly among you.* (1 Cor 14:24)

Dr. Edmund Clowney has termed this "doxological evangelism." But evangelism, Bible exposition, fellowship, and church business are not the purposes or ends for which the worship assembly takes place, and must not be allowed to warp the service into something it is not.[16]

On the other hand, we are not attempting to answer questions concerning how Bible conferences, fellowship suppers, church business meetings, or evangelistic meetings should be conducted outside of worship services. For example, generationally specific outreach events, such as puppet shows (for the young), soft-rock concerts (for yuppies), and Big-Band concerts (for the older folks) may be appropriate at other times. In other words, we are not attempting to say anything about what we might do the other six days of the week. We are only addressing what ought to go on in the commanded, and therefore obligatory, worship services of the Lord's day morning and evening.

Importance

So our question is, what *ought* (not what *can*) we (the *whole* congregation together) do in the *public* (not private) *worship* services (not in other congregational gatherings) of the Lord's Day?

How important is it that we answer this question? Let's put it this way: how important is worship? You may need to stop to think about it for a moment, and sort through the various activities of life. But even a superficial consideration will undoubtedly lead you to conclude that, of course, nothing we do is as important as worship; no, nothing of a secular nature, like work, play, or even family life. Not even religious activities such as evangelism, fellowship, charity, or private spiritual disciplines are as important. There can be no more important question for us to answer than this one.

---

[16] Frame repeatedly appeals to the Great Commission as the determining factor in ordering worship (*Worship*, 146-147, 150).

In the primary text which we shall be examining, Jesus says that the Father "seeks" true worshipers (John 4:23). Thus does Jesus sum up the saving activity of the Father. What is the Father doing through the gospel? What is He doing through His Son? What is the point of the incarnation, the atonement, and the whole of redemption? The Father is seeking worshipers! What an unusual and unanticipated way of speaking of such things. Yet there it is. Robert G. Rayburn points out that, "Nowhere in all the Scriptures do we read of God's seeking anything else from the child of God." The Bible does not tell us that God seeks witnesses, or servants, or contributors. What He seeks is worshipers. Rayburn continues, "it is not without real significance that the only time in the Scriptures when the word 'seek' is used of God's activity is in connection with seeking true worshipers."[17]

There is a true sense in which worship is what the Christian gospel is all about. The "eternal gospel" that we preach is summarized by the angel of Rev 14:7 as "Fear God, and give Him the glory . . . and worship Him." As we've seen, the whole Christian life is presented by the Apostle Paul as an act of worship in which we "present" to God our body as a "living and holy sacrifice." This is a "spiritual service of worship" (Rom 12:1). The point of the gospel is to make saints of sinners so that they might be worshipers. Notice how Jesus moves from the topic of worship to that of salvation in verse 22, "You worship that which you do not know; we worship that which we know, for salvation is from the Jews" (John 4:22). To be saved is to be delivered from the ignorance and oppression of idolatry. For the Jews to "know" the way of worship is to possess "salvation," no less. Granted we may not be accustomed to expressing this as sharply as we now are. But this is the clear teaching of the New Testament. The end or purpose of evangelism and missions is to create a people to worship God. The disciples of Christ are "living stones," who

---

[17] *O Come Let Us Worship*, 15, 16.

are "being built up as a spiritual house for a holy priesthood, to offer up spiritual sacrifices acceptable to God through Jesus Christ" (1 Pet 2:5; cf. Eph 2:18-22). God creates "a people for (His) own possession" so that they "may proclaim the excellences of Him who has called (them) out of darkness into His marvelous light" (1 Pet 2:9). This is what the Christian mission, the Christian life, and Christian worship are all about. John Piper summarizes our point well,

> Missions is not the ultimate goal of the church. Worship is. Missions exist because God is ultimate, not man. When this age is over, and the countless millions of the redeemed fall on their faces before the throne of God, missions will be no more. It is a temporary necessity. But worship abides forever.[18]

Worship is our "ultimate priority," as the title of a recent book on the subject declares. Every child of God should know this.

Not only does the Bible emphasize the importance of worship, but the Reformed and Presbyterian heritage does as well. Many modern historians of the Reformation period have allowed the dominant personality of Luther and his struggle to faith to overshadow the heart of the Swiss and Calvinistic Reformation. For Luther and the Lutherans the focus was justification. "How may a man be just before God?" was their primary question. But for Zwingli, Calvin, and the "Reformed" stream, the focus was not justification, as important as they agreed it was. Their focus was worship. "How is God to be worshiped?" they asked. For Lutherans the enemy of faith was works. For the Reformed, the enemy of faith was idolatry.

Carlos M. N. Eire, in his acclaimed *War Against the Idols*, reminds our generation of that which the older historians were aware. "The central focus of Reformed Protestantism was its

---

[18] John Piper, *Let the Nations Be Glad: The Supremacy of God in Missions* (Grand Rapids: Baker Books) p. 17.

interpretation of worship . . ." Distinguishing Lutherans from Zwinglians he says,

> The main difference is that, for the Zwinglians, the Reformation decision consisted not so much in finding a just God, but rather in turning away from idolatry to the true God.[19]

The same may be said of the work of Heinrich Bullinger (Zwingli's successor at Zurich), Martin Bucer in Strassburg, William Farel in Neuchatel, and later with John Calvin in Geneva. The Reformation spread as these men and others preached against the idolatry of Medieval worship, and the people responded in iconoclastic rage. Windows were smashed, relics desecrated, statues shattered, altars chopped up, and churches whitewashed. Farel, says Eire, "used the images and the Mass as a focus for the process of Reformation."[20] At Geneva during the early years of reform, "the focus of attention was not the issue of justification, but rather that of the mass and the images, and all their attending 'abuses'."[21] Both Farel and Calvin describe their conversions not as rescues from works-righteousness, but from idolatry. Like the Thessalonians, they had "turned from idols to serve a living and true God" (1 Thess 1:9).

In his 1543 tract entitled *On the Necessity of Reforming the Church*, Calvin lists the two defining elements of Christianity which, in his words, constitute "the whole substance of Christianity." Those two elements are "a knowledge first, of the right way to worship God; and secondly of the source from which salvation is to be sought."[22] W. Robert Godfrey comments, "Remarkably Calvin put worship ahead of salvation in his list of

---

[19] Carlos M. N. Eire, *War Against the Idols* (Cambridge: Cambridge University Press, 1986), 2, 85.

[20] Ibid., 119.

[21] Ibid., 143.

[22] Ibid., 126; (also found in *Selected Works of John Calvin*, vol. 1, 126).

the two most important elements of biblical Christianity."[23] Eire comments further,

> Calvin defines the place of worship as none of his predecessors had done before . . . Worship, he says, is *the* central concern of Christians. It is not some peripheral matter, but 'the whole substance' of the Christian faith . . . One may even argue that it becomes the fundamental defining characteristic of Calvinism.[24]

What is the point of Biblical and theological study, of evangelism and missions, of knowing God and indeed of the whole Christian religion? The answer to all of the above is *worship*. The true knowledge of God leads to right worship which leads to right living. The Reformation divines preached *Soli Deo Gloria* in every sphere of life because they first sought it in worship.

> By making worship a necessary existential component of knowledge, Calvin turns it into the nexus between thought and action, between theology and its practical application. It is a very practical sort of theology that Calvin develops as a result of this. Religion is not merely a set of doctrines, but rather a way of worshiping, and a way of living.[25]

Not only on the continent of Europe, but in Great Britain as well, the heart of the battle between the followers of Calvin and the Anglican establishment was the issue of worship. For a hundred years the Puritans struggled to reform the Prayer Book along Genevan lines, culminating in Civil War, the calling of the Westminster Assembly, and Parliamentary approval of the

---

[23] Robert W. Godfrey, "Calvin and the Worship of God," (unpublished manuscript, n.d.).

[24] Carlos M. N. Eire, *War Against the Idols*, 232, 233.

[25] Ibid., 232.

Directory for the Public Worship of God for the kingdoms of England, Scotland, Wales, and Ireland.

No, we are not accustomed to thinking in this way today. The current situation, where even churches which identify themselves as heirs of the Reformation, such as the PCA, and which, in the name of freedom, fail to provide Directories for Worship, could not be more ironic. Few have the stomach for careful thinking about worship. Fewer still see the need for it. Not only do many see no connection between *doctrine* and practical living, but still more see no connection between *worship* and practical living. So why regulate worship since, as is generally assumed, it would only divide, and isn't so important anyway? We tend to be like Calvin's detractors, who accused him of fracturing the unity of the church over trifles. Like his detractors, however, we are wrong about this. Questions about how to worship God are the most important of all, in their own right, and in their far-reaching application.

Worship Begins with God

John 4 may serve as the primary text for our discussion of worship. Remember the setting. Jesus encounters the Samaritan woman at the well. He offers her living water, which she wants. But then Jesus brings up her current living arrangements. She has had five husbands and is now living with a man not her husband. Trapped, she then diverts the direction of the conversation away from morality to religion, asking if the right place of worship is in Samaria or Jerusalem. She says, "Our fathers worshiped in this mountain, and you people say that in Jerusalem is the place where men ought to worship" (John 4:20). His startling answer is, "Woman, believe Me, an hour is coming when neither in this mountain, nor in Jerusalem, shall you worship the Father." Jesus partially sides with the Jews in that debate saying,

> You worship that which you do not know; we worship
> that which we know, for salvation is from the Jews.
> (John 4:22)

Knowledge counts. Truth counts. Samaritan worship was in

error. Samaritans and, by implication, all people, must look to the Jews, and in particular the book of the Jews, the Bible, in order to learn how to worship God and thus possess salvation. But then He repeats the substance of verse 21 by adding,

> But an hour is coming, and now is, when the true worshipers shall worship the Father in spirit and truth; for such people the Father seeks to be His worshipers. God is spirit, and those who worship Him must worship in spirit and truth. (John 4:23, 24)

I believe that this is the single most revolutionary statement that Jesus ever made. Clearly He is saying that the *place* of worship no longer matters, rather the *spirit*. He is marginalizing the *externals* of worship while giving prominence to the *internal*. Jerusalem, remember, was important because the temple was there, and with the temple, the altars, the priests, and the sacrifices. If the *place* of worship is no longer significant, the whole Old Testament system is being swept away. Typological Old Testament worship, with its symbols of our Great High Priest and the Lamb of God who would take away the sin of the world, is abolished with a word and contrasted with that which shall stand in its place. Over against that which is temporary, typological, and external shall be new covenant worship offered in "spirit and truth." What does this mean? It means this: over against Samaritan errors, worship must be "in truth," that is, according to God's revelation of truth; over against concern for the externals of place and procedure, worship must be "in spirit," that is, a matter of the right spirit, of the heart, of the motive.

What theological justification is given for these sweeping changes?

Notice the only explanatory word that Jesus gives here, beyond the bare assertion that the changes are coming, is "God is spirit" (v 24). This single statement alone provides the foundation, the orientation, the perspective from which all the rest flows. Worship begins with the doctrine of God. Because God is "spirit" our worship "must" be in "spirit and truth." The "mustness" of worship is the direct result of the unchanging nature of God. Worship must be as Jesus says it must be because God is who He is. There is a true sense in which we can say nothing more important about worship than this. There is but one God. That God is "spirit." The essential questions about worship are answered in relation to Him. If we start our discussion about worship on some other foot, then we are on the wrong foot. We must follow Jesus on this. The Samaritans and Jews were having their own "worship wars." Questions about worship are answered not with reference to Jews and Samaritans or any other people group. The critical issues all flow from the existence and nature of God. This is to say that in a sense more profound than we may have considered, worship is *for God*. We do not worship utterly without consideration for the congregation. The Apostle Paul's concern for edification in 1 Cor 14 makes that clear. But the primary concern in worship is that which God wants or requires. Indeed what the people of Samaria or Jerusalem might find meaningful or appealing is not raised by Jesus even as a consideration. The critical issue is God, His nature, and His demands. We take "God is spirit" as a critical orienting principle which shall guide us through the remainder of this discussion. Because God is spirit, the external and typological emphasis of Old Testament worship must be of necessity *temporary*. Worship must be "in spirit." Because God is spirit, worship must also be practiced with integrity, with faithfulness to God's self-revelation, it must be "in truth."

We shall deal with the latter and then with the former. But before we do we should note that there are two sides to worship, and we "must" get them both right. There is the *heart* of worship (its spirit) and its *content* and *form* (its truth). Both are necessary. Both are commanded. Periodically the question is raised, "Are you saying that God isn't pleased with the worship of such and such group of very earnest, sincere, devout Christians?" The answer we give is that form is not irrelevant. God cares about the form and content of worship as well as its spirit. One may be very sincere, and yet sincerely wrong, offering to God worship in a form that He has not authorized. The extreme case of this is found in pagan worship, such as the worship of the prophets of Baal on Mount Carmel, who practiced self-mutilation amidst their ceremonial dance and frenzied cries (1 Kgs 18:25-29). Were they earnest, sincere, devout? Absolutely. Likewise the ancient Canaanites offered their infants to Molech in human sacrifice. A more zealous expression of religious devotion can scarcely be imagined. But the form was utterly unauthorized, uncommanded, and wrong.

Form matters. Jesus says worship *must* be conducted with both the right *attitude* and the right *form*, with both spirit and truth.

2. WORSHIP "IN TRUTH"

W E WILL TAKE THE TWO PRIMARY PRINCIPLES OF BIBLICAL worship in reverse order, beginning with "truth," and then considering "spirit." Jesus says worship must be "in truth." This should be understood in two senses.

According to Scripture

First, worship that is "in truth" is according to Scripture. The Samaritans were no different than the rest of humanity. "You worship that which you do not know," Jesus told the Samaritan woman. There are almost limitless ways in which God might be worshiped. Jesus is insisting that we get it right. We must worship God according to His self-revelation. If we are to worship in *truth*, we must submit to scriptural revelation.

Calvin argued that "lawful" worship is that which He has established "by Himself."[26] He called for "the rejection of any mode of worship that is not sanctioned by the command of God."[27] This principle has become known as "the regulative principle."[28] The Catholic, Lutheran, and Anglican understanding may be called a "normative principle" – general norms are given but whatever is not expressly forbidden by

---

[26] John Calvin, *Institutes of the Christian Religion* (Philadelphia: The Westminster Press, 1960) II.8.17.

[27] John Calvin, "On the Necessity of Reforming the Church" in *Selected Works of John Calvin*, Vol. 1, (Baker Book House, 1983 [1844]), 133.

[28] One approaches despair when Frame distinguishes his methodology from the Puritans as simply "obeying everything that God says in Scripture about worship." Again, "we must simply search the Scriptures to determine what is appropriate and inappropriate to do when the church meets together as a body in the name of the Lord Jesus." (*Worship*, 54, 55). What, if not this, has Reformed Protestantism been aiming at for the past 480 years?

Scripture in worship is permitted. The Reformed practice was much more rigorous. It stated that whatever is not enjoined by Scripture (whether by command, example, or by deduction from broader principles) is forbidden. *The Westminster Confession of Faith* expressed it in this way:

> But the acceptable way of worshiping the true God is instituted by himself, and so limited by his own revealed will, that he may not be worshiped according to the imaginations and devices of men, or the suggestions of Satan, under any visible representation, or any other way not prescribed in the holy Scripture. (Chapter XXI. 1)

Where does the Bible teach this? Certainly the point is made in the very detailed prescriptions for worship found in Exodus 25-40 and Leviticus, but also in the following:

- Cain and Abel (Gen 4:3-8) – this was the first "worship war." Abel offers "the firstlings of his flock and their fat portions," but Cain offers "the fruit of the ground." The Lord "had regard for Abel and for his offering; but for Cain and for his offering He had no regard." Why? The Lord's rebuke, "If you do well, will not your countenance be lifted?" implies that either the spirit or truth of the offering was deficient. It was either an unauthorized offering or an authorized offering offered in the wrong way.

- *The Second Commandment* (Exod 20:4) – in prohibiting worship through images, God declares that He alone determines how He is to be worshiped. Though their use be ever so sincere and sensible (as aids to worship) images are not pleasing to Him, and by implication, *neither is anything else that He has not sanctioned.*

- *The Golden Calf* (Exod 32) – probably a representation of Jehovah (see vv 4, 5, 8), but totally unacceptable for use in worship because unauthorized.

- *Nadab and Abihu* (Lev 10) – they offer up "strange fire" to the Lord, that is, an offering offered in a manner "which He had not commanded them" (10:1), and God struck them dead. In so doing God made a statement to the ages – "By those who come near Me I will be treated as holy . . ." (10:2,3), which could only mean those who approach God must do so in a way consistent with what He has commanded.

- *Warnings not to add to or take away* from God's commandments (Deut 4:2; 12:32)
- The *rejection of Saul's unprescribed worship,* and the principle "obedience is better than sacrifice" (1 Sam 15:22). Obedience to what? Obedience to God's commands regarding worship.
- The *rejection of pagan rites* "which I never commanded or spoke of, nor did it ever enter My mind" (Jer 19:6; 32:35). We may deduce that the rites performed in Israel were only to be those that God had spoken of or commanded.
- Jesus' *rejection of Pharisaic worship,* citing the words of Isaiah who said, "in vain do they worship Me, teaching as their doctrines the precepts of men" (Mark 7:7, cf. Matt 15:9, Isa 29:13).
- The *rejection of Samaritan worship* by Jesus since they worship "what (they) do not know" (John 4:22). "True" worship is impossible for them as long as they devise their own worship. Worship that is in "truth" is based upon the knowledge of what God has commanded.
- The *rejection of what the old divines called "will worship,"* translated in a modern version of Colossians as "the commandments and teachings of men . . . self-made religion and self-abasement and severe treatment of the body," all, no doubt sincere religious practices, but unacceptable because humanly devised (Col 2:22, 23 NASV).
- The regulating of prayer, singing, preaching, the Lord's Supper, the role of women, and the insistence on orderliness and decorum in 1 Corinthians 11–14, as well as the insistence on uniform and catholic practice (1 Cor 1:2; 4:17; 11:16; 14:33; Eph 4:4ff.).

This is just a sampling of the passages, and others could be cited. Clearly they teach that we are not free to improvise in our worship. Calvin warns of the "snares of novelty." But the regulative principle is rooted not merely in the above proof-texts, but is the necessary implication of the fundamental principles of Reformed theology. The rejection of the regulative principle would necessarily involve compromising central tenets of the Reformed faith. Consider the following outline, first suggested in the writings of T. David Gordon:

- *The Doctrines of God and Man* – no system of theology has given as much emphasis to the creator/creature distinction as has Biblical Calvinism. None has appreciated and celebrated the great gulf between the infinite God of heaven and earth and finite man. His thoughts are not our thoughts and His ways are not our ways (Isa 55:8,9). "Who has known the mind of the Lord?," the Apostle Paul asks (Rom 11:33). The creature cannot know what worship will be pleasing to God apart from His self-revelation. Isn't this the obvious implication of a Reformed view of the natures of God and man?

- *The Doctrine of Sin* – again, no system of theology has emphasized the extent of the effects of the fall on human nature as has the Reformed faith. *Total depravity* has been the phrase that we have used to describe the corruption of all of man's faculties, mind, will, and affections. "The hearts of the sons of men are full of evil," says Ecclesiastes (9:3). "The heart is more deceitful than all else and is desperately sick," says Jeremiah (17:9). There is none righteous . . . there is none who does good . . . there is none who seeks for God" (Rom 3:10-12). The *Westminster Confession of Faith* says of the fall that Adam and Eve and their posterity were "wholly defiled in all the parts and faculties of soul and body" and "are utterly indisposed, disabled, and made opposite to all good, and wholly inclined to evil" (VI. 2,4). It has never been stated more strongly than this, or more accurately. The effect of this radical corruption of man is to take us beyond the finite's ignorance of the infinite just discussed, to the positive principle of idolatry. Man is by nature an idolater (Rom 1:18-32). He cannot and will not get it right. The human heart is a "factory" of idols, said Calvin. We are not competent to devise God-honoring worship. If we follow our natural, even common-sense indications we will get it exactly wrong. A humble appreciation of this requires that we look to God to tell us that which He desires from us.

- *The Doctrine of Scripture* – no tradition has elevated the authority and sufficiency of Scripture to the heights that the Reformed tradition has. *Sola Scriptura* is a fundamental principle of the whole Protestant and Reformed heritage. Our final authority in all matters of faith and conduct is Scripture. "The supreme judge by which all controversies of religion are to be determined . . . can be no other but the Holy Spirit speaking in the Scripture" (WCF I. 10). For this task of ordering faith and life the Scripture is sufficient. The Apostle Paul writes,

> *All Scripture is inspired by God and profitable*
> *for teaching, for reproof, for correction, for*
> *training in righteousness; that the man of God*
> *may be adequate, equipped for every good*
> *work.* (2 Tim 3:16,17)

The saints are adequately equipped for "every good work" by Scripture. It teaches, reproves, corrects, and trains us for life's tasks. Through Scripture alone we are "thoroughly equipped" (NIV) for "every," not some or most, but *every* good work." The all-important work of worship would not only be included, but would be at the top of any list of works for which Scripture is designed to equip us. Again, we cite the *Confession,*

> The whole counsel of God, concerning all things
> necessary for His own glory, man's salvation, faith,
> and life, is either expressly set down in Scripture,
> or by good and necessary consequence may be
> deduced from Scripture: unto which nothing at
> any time is to be added. (I.6).

- *The Doctrine of the Church* – the Reformed tradition has sharply limited the church's authority and power to those areas specifically delegated to it by Christ. Its authority is extensive (the "keys" of Matt 16:18ff; 18:18ff) yet is "ministerial and declarative." It may administer what Christ calls it to administer, and it may declare what Christ calls it to declare, argues T. David Gordon, "but it does not have discretionary power to frame new ordinances or laws."[29] The church may not "bind the conscience" by creating rules not addressed or implied by Scripture. The regulative principle is the necessary expression of this principle in the area of worship. In the church's worship it may require of its members only that which Christ requires, that and no more. Thus the people are free from the traditions and devices of mere men.

Perhaps the *doctrine of God's sovereignty*, the doctrine which does so much to give substance and shape to Reformed thought, best summarizes our point. Because our God is a sovereign God, He is sovereign over His worship. He alone *can* rightly order His worship (because we are finite and fallen), and He alone *does* order His worship (through His word to which His church is subject). He is not obligated to accept whatever worship finite and fallen man might devise, or even what redeemed ecclesiastical officials might create. He is Lord. He is sovereign. He alone *can* and *does* authorize the worship that pleases Him.

Thus we do in worship that which is "according to Scripture." We limit ourselves to those things which He Himself has authorized and has promised to bless. This is not an odious or burdensome requirement. It is simply a matter of embracing those activities or elements in worship that God has authorized and to which He has attached His promises. The regulative principle flows necessarily from the whole system of Reformed Theology.

---

[29] T. David Gordon, "Presbyterian Worship: Its Distinguishing Principle," (unpublished manuscript, n.d.)

Elements, Forms, Circumstances

This then leads to the question, what specifically has He authorized? What are the *elements* which He has ordained for worship? The *Confession* provides specifics –

> Prayer with thanksgiving . . . the reading of the Scriptures with godly fear, the sound preaching and conscionable hearing of the Word . . . singing of psalms with grace in the heart . . . the due administration and worthy receiving of the sacraments instituted by Christ, are all parts of the ordinary religious worship of God. (XXXI. 3, 5)

In addition, it speaks of occasional elements such as "religious oaths" and "vows" (as in Creeds, membership covenants, and ordination vows) as legitimate parts of "religious worship" (XXI.5, XXII.1). Texts such as Acts 2:42 provide a glimpse of the early church in worship, in simple services of the word, sacraments, and prayer. We also see the Apostle Paul regulating prayer (1 Cor 11:2-16; 14:14-17; 2 Tim 2:1-3), the singing of praise (1 Cor 14:26, 27; Col 3:16; Eph 5:19), the ministry of the word (1 Cor 14:29-33; 1 Tim 4:13; 2 Tim 4:1, 2), the collection (1 Cor 16:1, 2), and the Lord's Supper (1 Cor 11:17-34). These would all appear to be regular elements of the worship of the apostolic church. *Prayer*, the *reading of Scripture*, the *preaching of Scripture*, the *singing of Psalms*, the administration of the *sacraments*, and *religious oaths* are all "according to Scripture," modeled by apostolic example, regulated by apostolic command, and accompanied by divine promises of blessing.

At this point, a detractor might ask about pulpits and hymn books and lights and microphones and question the consistency with which the regulative principle is being applied. Where, one might ask, is the Scriptural warrant for these innovations? The Reformed tradition generally, and *The Westminster Standards* specifically, distinguish between *elements* (which are Scripturally determined and unchanging), *forms* (the contents of the elements, regarding which there is considerable freedom), and *circumstances*, which are governed by broader considerations. For example, the *element* of prayer may be expressed through a written or extemporaneous *form*. The *element* of preaching may be textual or topical in *form*. The *element* of Scripture reading may be expressed in various *forms*: a few verses or a chapter or more, from Genesis or Revelation, or from anywhere in between. In each of the cases the *form* is the content and structure through which the *element* is expressed. Forms are not limitless. A form must be consistent with the nature of the element. One may not "dance the sermon" primarily because a sermon by nature is spoken communication. Dance is not a form of preaching, but a new element, the arguments of their proponents notwithstanding.[30] Still, there are a range of choices. T. David Gordon acknowledges that this category "appears to be less well-known than the categories "element" or "circumstance." Nevertheless, it has been an important part of the discussion of worship since the Reformation. For example, Calvin assembled a *Form of Church Prayers* (1542), the *Larger Catechism* and scores of Reformed authors since have referred to the Lord's Prayer as a *form* of prayer, and various *forms* of family prayer and public prayer have been published over the years. Also, a debate over "free" versus "fixed" *forms* of worship has been carried on by Presbyterians since the days of the Puritans. A cursory acquaintance with the literature of classical Protestantism will verify this claim. "Form" is the word traditionally used to identify the content of an element and the way it is structured.[31]

---

[30] Frame sees drama as "a form of preaching and teaching," pointing out that "biblical preaching and teaching contain many dramatic elements" (*Worship*, 93). This is a classic case of the argument of the beard. Preaching and drama do lie upon a spectrum as do clean shaves and beards. There are dramatic sermons and sermonic dramas even as there are six-o'clock shadows and light beards. But a clean shave is not a beard and a sermon is not a skit. We can distinguish between these things and speak meaningfully of the difference.

[31] Gordon provides the following support: "*Larger Catechism* Question 186 says: 'The whole Word of God is of use to direct us in the duty of prayer; but the special rule of direction is that *form* of prayer which our Savior Christ

31

Circumstances are addressed by the *Confession* in I.6:
there are some circumstances concerning the
worship of God . . . common to human actions
and societies, which are to be ordered by the light
of nature and Christian prudence, according to
the general rules of the Word, which are always
to be observed.

The "light of nature," "Christian prudence," and "general
rules of the word" are to help us resolve circumstantial issues
that are "common to human actions and societies," that is,
common to public gatherings. For example, all public assemblies
must resolve the questions of illumination, of sound projection
or amplification, of meeting time and place, and if group singing
or reciting is to take place, of how to provide texts for the group.

---

taught His disciples, commonly called the Lord's Prayer.' Again, *Shorter
Catechism* Question 99 says: 'The whole Word of God is of use to direct us
in prayer; but the special rule of direction is that *form* of prayer which Christ
taught His disciples, commonly called the Lord's Prayer.' Similarly, the
following directions from the Directory of Worship of the Presbyterian
Church in America would find parallels in the older, earlier forms of
government from which these statements had been derived:

"47.6. The Lord Jesus Christ has prescribed no fixed *forms* for public worship
but, in the interest of life and power in worship, has given His Church a
large measure of liberty in this matter. It may not be forgotten, however,
that there is true liberty only where the rules of God's Word are observed
and the Spirit of the Lord is, that all things must be done decently and in
order, and that God's people should serve Him with reverence and in the
beauty of holiness.

"52.4. Ministers are not to be confined to fixed *forms* of prayer for public
worship, yet it is the duty of the minister, previous to entering upon his
office, to prepare and qualify himself for this part of his work, as well as for
preaching.

"63.3. Family worship, which should be observed by every family, consists
in prayer, reading the Scriptures, and singing praises; or in some briefer
form of outspoken recognition of God."

T. David Gordon, "Some Answers Regarding the Regulative Principle,"
Westminster Theological Journal, Vol. 55.2, (Fall 1993), 326 n18.

How are they to be resolved? By using "Christian prudence" or sanctified common sense. We are not to expect Scripture-texts for these questions. Returning to the example of prayer, I may pray in worship (it is an authorized *element*), a free or written prayer (matters of *form*), using an unaided voice or a microphone (matters of *circumstance*). I may preach (element) from Mark's gospel or Luke's (form) in an assembly hall illuminated by electric lights or oil lamps (circumstances).

Thus there is a consistency in the application of the regulative principle, one which recognizes the important distinctions between *elements*, which require scriptural sanction (by command, example, or implication), freedom in *forms*, and common sense in *circumstances*. The regulative principle as outlined demonstrates what Reformed people have meant by worship, that is "according to Scripture." It summarizes the Reformed view of worship. Indeed it is "Calvinism at worship," as T. David Gordon has said. It is the historic principle by which the Reformed church has articulated its understanding of the command of Jesus that we worship "in truth."

Filled with Scripture

Second, worship "in truth" must be filled with Scripture. Worship is not only governed by the Word, but it is also saturated with the Word. The Samaritans don't "know" what they worship. Christians are to know. Old Testament worship expressed much of its truth in external, physical, typological form. The New Testament, with its spiritual worship, will not. The truth *expressed* will have greater emphasis in the new era because the truth *represented* will be diminished. The Bible provides both the *structure* and the *content* of our worship.

Christian worship is thoughtful and filled with content. Pagans pray with "meaningless repetition" and "many words" (Matt 6:7). This is typical. Pagan worship functions on the level of feeling and experience rather than thought. We are to love God with our minds (Matt 20:37). Our "spiritual service of worship" is offered with renewed minds (Rom 12:1, 2). As Calvin pointed out (and Augustine before him) herein lies "the difference between the singing of men and that of birds." The parrot and nightingale may sing beautifully, "but the unique gift of man is to sing knowing that which he sings."[32] Our "psalms, hymns, and spiritual songs" "teach and admonish" (Col 3:16). Our worship is a two-sided conversation in which God speaks to us intelligibly in His word, and we speak back intelligibly in words that He has taught us. Our minds are never to be "unfruitful." Rather, we are to "pray with the spirit" and "with the mind also." We are to "sing with the spirit" and "with the mind also" (1 Cor 14:14, 15). What God has joined together ought not ever to be broken asunder. The specific content with which our minds are to be occupied is that of Holy Scripture.

Thus our praise is modeled on Biblical Psalms, our confession of sin on Biblical repentance, our confession of faith on Biblical doctrines, and our preaching on Biblical texts. We address God intelligently (in Biblical praise and confession) and He addresses our understanding (through His Word). To put it simply, in worship we *pray* the Bible, *sing* the Bible, *read* the Bible, and *preach* the Bible and *see* the Bible (in the sacraments). The language of Christian worship is the language of Scripture. Why? Because this is what converts, sanctifies, and edifies God's people.

The Apostle Paul teaches that "faith comes from hearing the Word of God" (Rom 10:17). How are we born again? By the Word of God (1 Pet 1:23-25). How do we grow in Christ? By the "pure milk of the word" (1 Pet 2:2). How are we sanctified? "Sanctify them in the truth: Thy word is truth," Jesus said (John 17:17). Matured? Conformed to the image of God? By the Word of God performing its work in us (1 Thess 2:13). The gospel (*euangellion*) is the power of God (Rom 1:16; cf. 1 Cor 1:18, 24). The gospel message (*kerygma*) comes "in demonstration of the Spirit and power" (1 Cor 2:4). It comes "in power and in the Holy Spirit with full conviction" (1 Thess 1:5). Consequently, our worship is full of Biblical content.

---

[32] Preface to the Psalter, 1543.

34

One might have thought that this was obvious to anyone coming out of a Protestant evangelical background. Unfortunately, we can no longer count on this to be so. Biblical content is rapidly disappearing from evangelical worship. Some observers' attempts to evaluate "our time" by looking only at particular songs or sermons and asking, "what's wrong with this?"[33] We think that one must step back and look not at isolated examples and identify the *trajectory* of evangelical worship from a generation ago to today. A mere generation ago among Protestant evangelicals substantial portions of Scripture were read, sermons were expository, hymns were loaded with Biblical content, and prayers were full of Biblical content and allusions. Typically today little Scripture is read. Sermons are topical. Songs have comparatively little Biblical content, and what little there is of it is repeated with mantra-like frequency.[34] Prayers are short or non-existent, and are expressed with language that is overly-familiar, and underly-Biblical. The sacraments, which require considerable Biblical reading and explanation in order to be properly administered are infrequently observed or even moved to mid-week. Evangelical and Reformed Protestants cannot be

---

[33] John Frame's books are particularly deficient at this point. He spends much of his effort defending this or that song or practice, but never surveys the big picture. He never considers the trajectory. Where have we come in the evangelical world? Where are we going? It is impossible to give an adequate evaluation of the parts without considering the whole.

[34] David Wells has analyzed the theological content of the 406 songs of the two most popular contemporary songbooks, *Worship Songs of the Vineyard* and *Maranatha! Music Praise Chorus Book*. He compared them with the 662 hymns of *The Covenant Hymnal*. He summarized his findings, saying that "the large majority of praise songs I analyzed, 58.9 percent, offer no doctrinal grounding or explanation for the praise; in the classical hymnody examined it was hard to find hymns that were *not* predicated upon and did not develop some aspect of doctrine" (my emphasis). In addition, important Biblical themes are largely ignored. For example, the theme of the church is found in 1.2% of the songs; sin, penitence and longing for holiness in 3.6%; the holiness of God in 4.3%. *Losing Our Virtue* (Grand Rapids: Eerdmans, 1998), 44.

pleased about these developments. One need not be a prophet to sense trouble coming down the road. What shall we call "worship" when the Bible is not read, not preached, not sung, and not prayed except in token doses? Shall we call it a service? an event? a celebration? Since it is "sacred writings which are able to give (us) the wisdom that leads to salvation through faith which is in Christ Jesus," what kind of church will be left after a generation of "worship" in which these "sacred writings" are largely absent (2 Tim 3:15)?

We may outline our principles as follows:

- *Read the Bible* – The Westminster Assembly's *Directory for the Publick Worship of God* commends the reading of whole chapters of Scripture. Paul told Timothy, "devote yourself to the public reading of Scripture, to preaching and to teaching" (1 Tim 4:13). In Reformed worship we read not just a verse or two here and there, but extended passages of Scripture.

- *Preach the Bible* – "From the very beginning the sermon was supposed to be an explanation of the Scripture reading," says Hughes Old, arguing from Nehemiah 8. It "is not just a lecture on some religious subject, it is rather an explanation of a passage of Scripture."[35] "Preach *the word*," Paul tells Timothy (2 Tim 4:2). Expository, sequential, verse by verse, book by book, preaching through the whole Bible, the "whole counsel of God" (Acts 20:27), was the practice of many of the church fathers (e.g. Chrysostom, Augustine), all the Reformers and the best of their heirs ever since. The preached word is the central feature of Reformed worship.[36]

---

[35] Hughes O. Old, *Worship*, 59, 60.

[36] Remarkably Frame writes, "there is no specific Biblical command, so far as I can tell, to have sermons in worship" (Some Questions, *Westminster Theological Journal*, vol. 54 (1990), 366 n 10). One wonders about a brand of "biblicism" that considers it necessary to make such a statement. Where in all of the Bible do the people of God assemble and not read and explain

- *Sing the Bible* – Our songs should be rich with Biblical and theological content. The current divisions over music are at the heart of our worship wars. Yet some principles should be easy enough to identify. First, what does a Christian worship song look like? Answer, it looks like a Psalm. Reformed Protestants have sometimes exclusively sung Psalms. But even if that is not one's conviction, one should still acknowledge that the Psalms themselves should be sung and that the Psalms provide the model for Christian hymnody. If the songs we sing in worship look like Psalms, they will develop themes over many lines with minimal repetition. They will be rich in theological and experiential content. They will tell us much about God, man, sin, salvation, and the Christian life. They will express the whole range of human experience and emotion. Second, what does a Christian worship song *sound* like? Many are quick to point out that God has not given us a book of tunes. No, but He has given us a book of lyrics (the Psalms) and their form will do much to determine the kinds of tunes that will be used. Put simply, the tunes will be suited to the words. They will be sophisticated enough to carry substantial content over several lines and stanzas. They will use minimal repetition. They will be appropriate to the emotional mood of the Psalm or Bible-based Christian hymn. Sing the Bible. These ideas are worked out in more detail in *The Pastor's Public Ministry* (Greenville: Reformed Academic Press, 2001) 25-30.
- *Pray the Bible* – the pulpit prayers of Reformed churches should be rich in Biblical and theological content. Do we not learn the language of Christian devotion from

---

the Scripture? (e.g. Deut. 26:1ff; Exod 24:1-11; Neh 8:1-8; Luke 4:14-21; Acts 20:7ff; etc.) For an overwhelming case against Frame at this point, see Hughes O. Old, *The Reading and Preaching of the Scriptures in the Worship of the Christian Church*, Volumes 1 & 2 (Grand Rapids: Eerdmans, 1998).

the Bible? Do we not learn the language of confession and penitence from the Bible? Do we not learn the promises of God to believe and claim in prayer from the Bible? Don't we learn the will of God, the commands of God, and the desires of God for His people, for which we are to plead in prayer, from the Bible? Since these things are so, public prayers should repeat and echo the language of the Bible throughout. This was once widely understood. Matthew Henry[37] and Isaac Watts[38] produced prayer manuals that trained Protestant pastors for generations to pray in the language of Scripture, and are still used today. Hughes Old has produced a similar work in recent years.[39]

- *See the Bible* – Augustine first referred to the sacraments as the "visible word." They are accompanied by extensive Bible reading (e.g. the words of institution and warning) and theological explanation (e.g. the covenant and the nature of the sacraments). They are themselves visual symbols of gospel truths. In Reformed worship the word and sacrament are never separated. Why? For that matter, why read, preach, sing, and pray the Bible? Because faith comes by *hearing* the word of God (Rom 10:17).

Thus the worship of Reformed Protestantism is *simple*. We merely read, preach, pray, sing and see the Word of God, but more about its simplicity later. Sometimes this emphasis on the Bible in Reformed worship has been criticized as being overly "cognitive" or "intellectual,"[40] as well as anti-emotional and

---

[37] J. Ligon Duncan III (ed.), Matthew Henry's *A Method for Prayer* (Greenville: Reformed Academic Press, 1994).

[38] Isaac Watts, *A Guide to Prayer* (1715; reprint, Edinburgh: The Banner of Truth Trust: 2001).

[39] Hughes O. Old, *Leading in Prayer* (Grand Rapids: Eerdmans, 1995).

[40] Robert Webber and John Frame both typically say things like this. "For centuries the focus of Protestant thought about worship has been on worship as a cerebral act," says Webber. "What made worship worship was the sermon," (Robert Webber, "Reaffirming the Arts," *Worship Leader*, vol. 8,

against the arts. While this is not the place to take on all these issues (e.g. a theology of art, a theory of human psychology, a philosophy of learning, etc.), we would simply answer: worship must be "according to Scripture." In addressing the understanding, Scripture addresses the whole man, mind, will and emotions. Scripture-filled sermons, songs, and prayers are not "cerebral" or "academic," any more than a human father's loving and firm communication to his beloved child can be so classified. It is odd that it should have even come to be considered such.

The regulative principle is not difficult. It is not heavy or burdensome. It merely requires that we worship "according to Scripture." We are to both structure our worship with Biblical elements, and fill those elements with Biblical content.

Those who attend a Reformed worship service will hear a steady stream of sanctifying Biblical content. They will be *called to worship* with a Biblical call such as Psalm 95:

> Come, let us worship and bow down; Let us kneel before
> the Lord our Maker. For He is our God, And we are
> the people of His pasture, and the sheep of His hand.
> Today, if you would hear His voice, (Ps 95:6, 7)

They will sing an opening *hymn of praise* that is rich with Biblical language and themes. They will hear an *invocation* that echoes the language of Biblical praise such as that found in 1 Timothy 1:17 and 6:15-16:

> Now to the King eternal, immortal, invisible, the only
> God, … the blessed and only Sovereign, the King of

---

no. 6, November/December, 1999, 10). Also Frame, *Worship*, 77-78. Frame is concerned that traditional hymns have *too much* Biblical/theological content. For example, "'Shine, Jesus Shine' stands up pretty well against 'Of the Father's Love Begotten'" says Frame, because the latter "states too many doctrines to fast to be truly edifying" (*Contemporary*, 116). By this standard, one supposes that the Psalms could never be sung, or, for that matter, the book of Romans could never be read (too many doctrines flying by too fast). He regularly biases his argument by referring to the "intellectual content" of songs and sermons rather than the Biblical content, the real point (*Contemporary*, 98ff).

> kings and Lord of lords; who alone possesses
> immortality and dwells in unapproachable light; whom
> no man has seen or can see. To Him be honor and
> eternal dominion!

They will recite a summary of Biblical doctrine in the language in one of the *historic creeds*. They will hear the Biblical language of confessions thanksgiving, and intercession in the "*pastoral prayer*." A significant portion of each testament will be *read*, and a complete *Psalm* (or large section of a longer Psalm) will be *sung*. The *sermon* will be an exposition of Scripture. The *closing hymn*, like the opening one, will be rich in Biblical language and allusion. Finally they will hear a Biblical *benediction*, such as the Aaronic:

> The Lord bless you and keep you,
> The Lord make His face to shine upon you,
>   and be gracious unto you
> The Lord lift up His countenance upon you
>   and give you His peace (Num 6:24-26)

Do not underestimate the cumulative impact of this weight of Scripture week in and week out throughout the life of the members of Reformed churches.

It should be clear by this point that the real battleground today is not over *elements* but *forms*. Only a small minority of Reformed churches believe that dance and drama are legitimate elements of worship, and an even smaller minority will ever implement their use. Even the newest of New School theologians continue to affirm the regulative principle. The real debate is whether contemporary forms are adequate for the expression of the Reformed faith. Can contemporary buckets carry Calvinistic water? Can an informal casual setting and tone, pop/rock music, minimal prayer and Bible reading, and needs-based topical preaching produce a new generation of Puritans, Huguenots, and Covenanters, that is, brave, uncompromising souls who will shape civilizations? Since it is in our Sunday public services that Reformed convictions receive their widest dissemination, *is it likely* that in those churches that have abandoned traditional forms for contemporary alternates that we will see reproduced in our generation the characteristics that were typical of Reformed people of previous generations, namely a warm piety (because they look gratefully to Christ alone); moral precision (because they hold to the third use of the law); steadfastness in hardship (because they believe in Romans 8:28 and the sovereignty of God); strong families (because they are aware of their covenantal responsibilities); and self-government (because Presbyterian government has taught them to regard the rights and responsibilities of the governed)? We are convinced that it will not happen precisely because contemporary forms are not up to the task. Only historically Reformed worship can do the job. Only Presbyterian buckets can carry Presbyterian water.

What ought we to do in worship? What has God promised to bless? The reading, preaching, singing and praying of the Scriptures, along the traditional lines outlined above, along with the sacraments Biblically explained and administered.

3. Worship "In Spirit"

J ESUS SAYS BECAUSE "GOD IS SPIRIT" WORSHIP MUST BE NOT ONLY "in truth," but also "in spirit." Remember Jesus is responding to the debate raised by the Samaritan woman. Her question is, where ought man to worship, "in this mountain" or "in Jerusalem" (v 20), in our building or yours, and by extension, according to this ritual or that? She is concerned with the externals of worship. He sides with the Jews (and Biblical revelation) regarding the truth content and form of worship. But as for the place, the location, the building? That now is irrelevant. "Neither," He says (v 21). The place and other externals of worship are *not* the issue any longer. If the building and location are insignificant, then what is significant? Internal matters are. In addition to being Biblical in structure and content, worship must also be conducted in the right "spirit." It is offered in the name of Jesus, who is the "truth" (John 14:6) and in the power of the Holy Spirit, apart from whom no one can say Jesus is Lord (1 Cor 12:3). The internal matters of worship, the intent, the motive, the intensity, the sincerity, the reverence, are the critical concerns.

Are we now adding something to the regulative principle? Not at all. Rather, the regulative principle is concerned with more than truth. We who care a great deal about formal correctness need to be careful about this. The very fact that few people today care about form means that those who do, in reaction to the banalities surrounding them, are vulnerable to the problem of making an idol out of correctness. Jesus, citing Isaiah before him, condemned the religious leaders of his day saying,

> *This people honors Me with their lips, but their heart*
> *is far away from Me.* (Matt 15:8)

What they were saying was fine. But their hearts were "far away," and consequently they worshiped "in vain." Both the *form* and *heart* of worship must be correct.

New Testament worship, prompted and inspired by the Holy Spirit, will be predominately spiritual and internal in ways that Old Testament worship was not. Here are the differences.

Internal or of the Heart

First, worship that is "in spirit" is from the heart. Because God is spirit He must be worshiped spiritually, internally, from the heart. When we sing we "make melody with (our) heart(s) to the Lord" (Eph 5:19; cf. Col 3:16). What is true of singing is true of all the elements. True worship is not a matter of sacred places but the spiritual condition of the heart. God's presence is in heaven. There are no holy buildings, holy places, or holy things through which God's blessing is uniquely mediated. Palestine is not a "Holy Land," where God is more present than other places. Our worship place is not "God's house," or a "sanctuary," as though God were more present in it than in other places. God has made no promises to convey His blessing in connection with the place or location of worship. We noticed that at the time of the dedication of Independent Presbyterian Church of Savannah's new church building in 1891 it was never called a "sanctuary." They called it a "church building" or "church house." God dwells in His people. They are the "living stones" which become "a spiritual house" for God (1 Pet 2:5, cf. Eph 2:19-22). The building only becomes a house for God when God's people are present within it. This seemed to be better understood a hundred years ago than it is today. The point for us is that worship can never be a matter of getting our bodies in the right building at the right time for the right ritual.

"What about the Old Testament?" we are repeatedly asked. "Didn't they have holy buildings, a holy land, and holy symbols?" Yes indeed they did, and Jesus abolished them. This is why it is crucial that the symbolic, typological and temporary nature of Old Testament worship be understood. Visual pictures were given to Israel of the spiritual realities that would be fulfilled in Christ. Lambs were sacrificed. Incense was burned. Blood was sprinkled.

Priestly garments were worn. Old Testament worship was prominently symbolic because it was pre-incarnational. Jerusalem, the temple, the priests, the altars, the incense and the sacrifices were the issue *then* because through them God provided pictures of the Christ who would come. These sense-stimulating types, however, were surpassed by the Antitype, Christ, who having come, is apprehended not by continuing types but by faith through His portrayal in the gospel. The types, in other words, were by design *temporary* and of necessity *inferior* to the revelation of the Antitype in the gospel.

Again, we must be careful not to overstate the case. The difference is one of emphasis. The New Testament sacraments are symbolic presentations of the gospel as well. They are "sensible signs" whereby "Christ and the benefits of the new covenant are represented" (*Shorter Catechism*). There is nothing inherently wrong with symbols. Likewise the Old Testament was not devoid of "spirit" and "truth." To maintain otherwise would be absurd. Of course there was great concern for spirit and truth in Old Testament worship. The symbols of the Old Testament were never ends in themselves, but were always meant to point to the internal and spiritual. The physical *temple* pointed to the Christian body and to the spiritual temple, the church (John 2:21). The sacrificial *lambs* pointed to the Lamb of God. The blood of bulls and goats (which could never put away sin) pointed ahead to the "precious blood, as of a lamb unblemished and spotless, the blood of Christ" (Heb 10:4; 1 Pet 1:19). The *priests* and their *garments* pointed to Christ, our great High Priest (Heb 2:17, 18). The "sacrifices of God" have always represented a "broken and contrite heart" (Ps 51:17).[41] The Old Testament worshiper aspires that "all that is

---

[41] Perhaps a parallel example may help. We read in John's gospel that "the law was given through Moses; grace and truth were realized through Jesus Christ," not because the Old Testament was all law and utterly devoid of grace and truth, or because the New Testament is all grace and utterly devoid of law, but as a matter of emphasis (John 1:17). Of course there was grace and truth then. But there was more emphasis on law in the Old Testament and grace in the New Testament. There is more truth now in that it is fuller and clearer in Christ.

within (him)" might "bless His holy name." (Ps 103:1) There was truth and spirit in the Old Testament, but not on the scale or with the clarity as in the New.

So what is the difference? It is a difference of emphasis and proportion. The Old Testament was loaded with symbols in anticipation of Christ. These symbols are by nature *temporary*. The New Testament has only two, baptism and the Lord's Supper. Thus the New Testament worship is "in spirit" in that it does not have the emphasis on symbols and types as did Old Testament worship.

Calvin's comments on John 4 are to the point:

> By these words (i.e. "in spirit") he meant not to declare that God was not worshiped by the fathers in this spiritual manner, but only to point out a distinction in the external form, viz., That while they had the Spirit shadowed forth by many figures, we have it in simplicity.[42]

Jesus, then, is emphasizing the *spirituality* of New Testament worship over against the symbolic and typological nature of the Old.

The church has at times succumbed to the temptation to return to typological worship and thought again of its ministers as priests, its buildings as temples, the Lord's Table as an altar, and the Lord's Supper as a sacrifice. It has added incense, processions, and clerical garb. Through ritual, ceremonies, art, pageantry, drama, dance, and sometimes music, it has sought to stimulate and inspire faith. This was exactly the thinking of the Medieval church, for which pictures were "the books of the unlearned." According to Philip Schaff, "sacred drama" was "fostered by the clergy and first performed in churches or the church precincts" and became "in some measure a medieval substitute for the sermon and the Sunday-School."[43] This

---

[42] John Calvin, "On The Necessity of Reforming the Church" in *Selected Works of John Calvin*, Vol.1 (Baker Book House, 1983 [1844]), 128.

[43] Philip Schaff, *History of the Christian Church*, vol. 5 (1907; reprint, Grand Rapids: W.B. Eerdman's, 1947), 869.

supplanting of the central role that the sermon played in the early church was a disastrous development in church history, as is every attempt to return to externalized Christian worship.

Let us summarize our conviction. Why would any movement in the direction of symbol over Spirit be seen negatively by the proponents of Biblical or Reformed worship? It would for the following reasons:

1. The Old Testament symbols were *temporary* by nature. The temple and everything in connection with it were only ever meant to fill a need for a time. They were a weak picture of the Messiah until His glory was "beheld" in Jesus Christ (John 1:14).

2. Symbols by nature are *inferior* to verbal revelation. This is why the church has no "dumb sacraments," as J. A. Motyer has put it. The sacraments are always accompanied by an explanatory word. They are not self-interpreting. They depend on the word in ways that the word does not depend on them. Thus the law, unlike God's revelation in Christ, is only a "shadow" and "not the very form of things" (Heb 10:1). Christ *is* the "very form of things." The point of the Book of Hebrews is that the church not go back to the Aaronic symbols and types (3:12 - 4:13; 6:1-8; 7-10, esp. 10:26-31; 11-13). You have the *form*, you don't need the *shadow*. Don't waste time looking at the shadow of your loved One when He Himself is standing there before you.

3. The addition of symbols beyond the two instituted by Christ are a *distraction* from the ordained means of grace. What Hughes Old said of the Reformers' attitude toward baptism is true of all worship generally:

> It was because the Reformers prized so highly the divinely given signs that they had such disdain for those signs of merely human intervention which obscured them.[44]

---

[44] Hughes O. Old, *The Shaping of the Reformed Baptismal Rite in the Sixteenth Century* (Grand Rapids: Eerdman's, 1992), 286.

4. Services dominated by symbols and accompanying rituals will tend toward *formalism*. The emphasis on the *external* in worship directs attention away from the *internal*, the heart and its motives, opening the door to soulless, heartless, rote worship.

Extraneous symbols, rituals and movements, harmless in themselves, perhaps even symbolically significant in the eyes of many, are to be avoided if they are not required by Scripture or immediately germane to the service itself. "A visually elaborate" setting, says Godfrey, "would interfere with our spiritual ascent binding our minds too much to earth."[45] Paul speaks of Jesus Christ being "publicly portrayed as crucified" before the "eyes" of the Galatians (Gal 3:1). This could only be a metaphorical reference to preaching. The gospel read and preached is a better portrayal of Christ than any material symbol. Unauthorized symbols avert attention and time away from those means (including the ordained symbols) which God has promised to bless. Remember, faith is the conviction of things "not seen" (Heb 12:1)! True faith comes through the word (Rom 10:17). True worship then must be primarily (though not absolutely) non-material, non-sensual, and non-symbolic. In true worship we ascend to God in heaven by faith. By faith we apprehend God on His throne of grace and worship Him there. By faith we see Christ in His gospel.

Thus, worship that is "in spirit" is from the heart. As we have noted, those of us who care the most about correctness in worship must never lose sight of the goal of worship: fellowship with God. What are we doing in worship? We are "drawing near" to God (Heb 4:15,16; 10:16- 22). We are coming into His presence (Jas (4:8-10). We are seeking and calling upon Him (Isa 55:6). Our great passion is to meet with our God. Our outlook must be that of the Psalmist,

---

[45] Robert W. Godfrey, "Calvin and the Worship of God," (unpublished manuscript, n.d.), 15.

*One thing I have asked from the Lord, that I shall
seek: That I may dwell in the house of the Lord all the
days of my life, To behold the beauty of the Lord,
And to meditate in His temple.* (Ps 27:4)

What is the one thing that he seeks above all else? That he
may "dwell in the house of the Lord" and "behold the beauty of
the Lord." Listen again,

*When Thou didst say, "Seek My face," my heart said
to Thee, "Thy face, O Lord, I shall seek."* (Ps 27:8)

It is God Himself that the Psalmist seeks through the forms of
Old Testament worship. The Old Testament saints longed for God's
personal presence even in and through their typological system.

*As the deer pants for the water brooks, So my soul
pants for Thee, O God. My soul thirsts for God, for
the living God;* (Ps 42:1,2)

*O God, Thou art my God; I shall seek Thee earnestly;
my soul thirsts for Thee, my flesh yearns for Thee, in
a dry and weary land where there is no water. Thus I
have beheld Thee in the sanctuary, to see Thy power
and Thy glory. Because Thy lovingkindness is better
than life, my lips will praise Thee. So I will bless Thee
as long as I live; I will lift up my hands in Thy name.
My soul is satisfied as with marrow and fatness, and
my mouth offers praises with joyful lips. When I
remember Thee on my bed, I meditate on Thee in the
night watches, for Thou hast been my help, and in
the shadow of Thy wings I sing for joy. My soul clings
to Thee; Thy right hand upholds me.* (Ps 63:1-8)

*Whom have I in heaven but Thee? And besides Thee,
I desire nothing on earth. My flesh and my heart may
fail, but God is the strength of my heart and my portion
forever. For, behold, those who are far from Thee
will perish; Thou hast destroyed all those who are
unfaithful to Thee. But as for me, the nearness of*

God is my good; I have made the Lord God my refuge, that I may tell of all Thy works. (Ps 73:25-28)

How lovely are Thy dwelling places, O Lord of hosts! My soul longed and even yearned for the courts of the Lord; My heart and my flesh sing for joy to the living God . . . How blessed are those who dwell in Thy house! They are ever praising Thee . . . For a day in Thy courts is better than a thousand outside. I would rather stand at the threshold of the house of my God, than dwell in the tents of wickedness. For the Lord God is a sun and shield; the Lord gives grace and glory; no good thing does He withhold from those who walk uprightly. O Lord of hosts, how blessed is the man who trusts in Thee! (Ps 84:1,2,4, 10-12)

Do you see the passion with which the Psalmist seeks for God, particularly in and through public worship? He "thirsts," seeks "earnestly," "yearns," and "clings." God's "lovingkindness" for him is "better than life." Besides God he desires "nothing on earth." God's "nearness" is his "good." God's "dwelling places" are "lovely" and he longs and yearns for them. Relish this deeply experiential language and do not settle for less. Come to God in Christ and feed upon the bread of life and quench the thirst of your soul with Living Water (John 6:35; 7:37).

This is what we ought to be doing week by week in our worship services. We are worshiping God in heaven whom we see there in all His glory through the eye of faith. This is why we emphasize preparation for worship. Our hearts must be right. Faith is critically important. Don't come to worship with one minute to spare. Don't think that all one need do is place one's body in the right building at the right time and where the right ritual is being performed. Arrive early. Pray your heart into a receptive condition. Ready yourself to see God by faith. God must be worshiped "in spirit," in the right spirit, with the right attitude.

Simple

Second, worship "in spirit" is simple. New Testament worship is devoid of procedural and ceremonial *complexity*. This follows closely on all that we have seen thus far of Biblical and spiritual worship. It is *simple*. It has no Jerusalem, and no Temple, no Levitical instructions. Once we say this we wish to clarify what we don't mean. Sometimes it is argued that because there is no Book of Leviticus, that is, no elaborate set of procedural instructions for worship in the New Testament, it must be that God has granted to the church the freedom to worship as it sees fit. "Calvin's response," to this argument, says Godfrey, "would be that the absence of a Levitical book in the New Testament reflects more the simplicity of the church's worship in Christ than creative freedom . . . the New Testament is full and complete as a guide and warrant for the simple worship of the children of God in the Spirit. No more freedom is given in the New Testament to invent forms of worship than was given in the Old."[46]

Detailed instructions in the New Testament would be appropriate if New Testament worship was meant to be elaborate in ritual, rich in symbolism, and complex in procedure. This was true of the Old Testament Levitical instructions which foreshadowed Christ. The Levitical priests were required to carry out their ministrations through detailed ritual, symbolism, and procedure. Let's remind ourselves of what was involved. The Old Testament required precise conformity to extensive and particular details regarding the externals of worship. These included the following:

- the *dimensions* of the tabernacle/temple (Exod 26-27; 1 Kgs 6-7, 2 Chr 3)
- The *furniture* of the tabernacle/temple including the curtains (Exod 26:1-14), boards and sockets (Exod 26:15-30), the ark of the covenant (Exod 25:10-22), the table

---

46 Ibid., 10, 11.

of showbread (Exod 25:23-30), the golden lampstand (Exod 25:31-46; Num 8:1-4), the veil and screen (Exod 26:31-37), the bronze altar (Exod 27:1-8); (cf. 1 Kgs 6; 2 Chr 4)

- *priestly garments* worn, including the breastpiece, ephod, robe, turban, sash and tunic (Exod 28, 30)
- *ritual details* including the consecration of priests (Exod 29:1-9, Lev 8, Num 8:1-22), the sacrifices (Exod 29:10-30, Lev 16:1-17:16, Lev 1-7; Num 28,29), the incense (Exod 30:1-21, 34-38), the priestly food (Exod 29:31-37), the anointing oil (Exod 30:22-23), the sacrificial animals (Lev 22:17-33), and other priestly regulations (Lev 21:1-22:16)
- *a schedule of regular offerings* including daily morning and evening (Exod 29:38-46; Num 28:1-8), weekly Sabbath (Num 28:9-10), and monthly (Num 28:11-15)
- *calendar* of Holy days, including Passover (Lev 16:29-34, 23:5; Num 28:16), Unleavened Bread (Lev 23:6-8; Num 28:17ff), First fruits (Lev 23:9-25; Num 28:16ff), the Day of Atonement (Lev 23:26-32; Num 29), and Booths (Lev 23:38-44)

Nothing parallels any of this anywhere in the New Testament. The closest New Testament ordinances to which we might point would be the sacraments of the Lord's Supper and baptism. But still we find nothing like the procedural details found in the Old Testament. Listen to just a small part of what was required of Aaron and the priests in offering atoning sacrifices.

> Aaron shall enter the holy place with this: with a bull for a sin offering and a ram for a burnt offering. He shall put on the holy linen tunic, and the linen undergarments shall be next to his body, and he shall be girded with the linen sash, and attired with the linen turban (these are holy garments). Then he shall bathe his body in water and put them on. And he shall take from the congregation of the sons of Israel two male goats for a sin offering and one ram for a burnt offering . . . And he shall take a firepan full of coals of fire

from upon the altar before the Lord, and two handfuls of finely ground sweet incense, and bring it inside the veil. And he shall put the incense on the fire before the Lord, that the cloud of incense may cover the mercy seat that is on the ark of the testimony, lest he die. Moreover, he shall take some of the blood of the bull and sprinkle it with his finger on the mercy seat on the east side; also in front of the mercy seat he shall sprinkle some of the blood with his finger seven times. (Lev 16:3-5, 12-14, etc.)

"Then he shall . . . and he shall . . . and he shall . . . and he shall," etc. Similar New Testament instruction might have been given. Ministers might have been commanded to begin services by sprinkling holy water, lighting incense, bowing to the east three times while crossing themselves and saying the "Our Father." A whole calendar of seasons and Holy days paralleling those of the Old Testament might have been given. In other words, a ritual of approach to God, with defined procedure, rich in symbolism, anchored to the calendar, might have been given. But there is none of this. This does not mean that the church is free to make of worship what it wishes. It does mean that our worship is to be simple, straightforward, without elaborate ritual, devoid of complex procedure, liberated from the calendar and nature's cycles, and limited in its use of symbols to those instituted by Christ, the Lord's Supper, and baptism. For the church to devise worship that is encumbered by ritual, symbolism, and procedure is to undermine the intent of God that our worship be simple, and return to the shadows of the Old Testament. Don't go there. Don't revive the pomp and circumstance of the medieval liturgies. Don't embrace the high-voltage extravaganzas of contemporary worship either. Don't create a new priesthood of technicians, artists, and actors. Our worship is simple and hence universally valid. It can be conducted and enjoyed at any place, at any time, whatever the income, education, or technological prowess of those involved. It can be conducted in an igloo in Alaska, a grass hut in the Congo, or in a grand cathedral in Paris. God may now be worshiped in Samaria or Jerusalem. We repeat the implication of Heb 8-10. The Levitical ordinances were "a copy and shadow of the heavenly things," but Christ "has obtained a more excellent ministry" (8:5, 6). The entrance of Christ into heaven itself, and not the earthly temple, "a mere copy of the true one," of necessity, means the abolition of the old "copy" (9:23ff). The Law, he says, was "only a shadow of the good things to come," which have come in Christ (10:1). He writes,

> Since therefore, brethren, we have confidence to enter the holy place by the blood of Jesus, by a new and living way which He inaugurated for us through the veil, that is, His flesh, and since we have a great priest over the house of God, let us draw near with a sincere heart in full assurance of faith, having our hearts sprinkled clean from an evil conscience and our bodies washed with pure water. (Heb 10:19-22)

His point is that we should not return to the complex symbols, rituals, and procedures by which the people of God approached God in the Old Testament. This way of worship has been abolished in Christ, who performed all the priestly and sacrificial tasks on our behalf, once for all. Our way is a "new and living way" of approach. Our sacrifice is "a sacrifice of praise to God, that is, the fruit of lips that give thanks to His name," not a material sacrifice following a prescribed procedure upon an altar (Heb 13:15). The glimpses of the church's worship provided in the New Testament bear out this point. The early Christians devoted themselves to "the apostles' teaching, and to fellowship, and to the breaking of bread, and to prayer" (Acts 2:42). They followed not the richly elaborate services of the temple, but the simple and unadorned worship of the synagogue. "They did not take over the rich and sumptuous ceremonial of the Temple," notes Hughes Old, "but rather the simpler synagogue service with its Scripture reading, its sermon, its prayers, and its psalmody."[47]

---

[47] Old, Worship, 43

Their services were simple services of the word, sacraments, and prayer. So should ours be.

The "style" of one's preaching provides a case study of how the early church understood the principle of simplicity. Addressing first-century Greeks given to excessive rhetorical flourishes, the Apostle Paul argues that the simplicity of the gospel requires simple packaging, lest the *means* of presentation contradict the *message*.

> For Christ did not send me to baptize, but to preach
> the gospel, not in cleverness of speech, that the cross
> of Christ should not be made void. (1 Cor 1:17)

"Cleverness" in speech, that is, a message dressed up in the sophisticated techniques of the Greek orators would "void" the cross. Think of Bible verses pasted to the midsections of belly-dancers (not too far-fetched; remember Larry Flynt's experiment combining centerfolds with Bible verses). Marshall McLuhan is right: the medium is the message. The medium can shout so loudly that the message gets buried. The Apostle Paul employed a simple style appropriate to a simple message:

> And when I came to you, brethren, I did not come
> with superiority of speech or of wisdom, proclaiming
> to you the testimony of God...and I was with you in
> weakness and in fear and in much trembling. (1 Cor
> 2:1, 3)

His simple style of proclamation was suited to the simple message of "Christ crucified":

> For I determined to know nothing among you except
> Jesus Christ, and Him crucified. (1 Cor 2:2)

He was careful to preach simply because only a simple style of speech would highlight the simplicity of the message, whereas a sophisticated style would undermine it:

> And my message and my preaching were not in
> persuasive words of wisdom, but in demonstration of
> the Spirit and of power, (1 Cor 2:4)

When unbelievers came to repent and believe, it would be not because the preacher was clever, not because He preached with "superiority of speech or of wisdom," or "in persuasive words of wisdom." Rather his simple style left the "demonstration of the Spirit and of power" in plain view,

> that your faith should not rest on the wisdom of men,
> but on the power of God. (1 Cor 2:5)

When the preaching style is simple, the positive response of faith is not a response to a man and his gifts, his charm, his worldly persuasiveness, but to the Spirit.

Listen to the Apostle Paul once again contrast "craftiness" and the clear "manifestation of the truth into every man's conscience."

> Therefore, since we have this ministry, as we received mercy, we do not lose heart, but we have renounced the things hidden because of shame, not walking in craftiness or adulterating the word of God, but by the manifestation of truth commending ourselves to every man's conscience in the sight of God. (2 Cor 4:1, 2)

Gospel preaching does not require tricks. It is simply the "manifestation of the truth" to the "conscience" of the listeners. If we are right in citing preaching as a case study in simplicity, then you can see the implications for each element of worship and for the whole service. Everything about our worship is to be simple. Nothing is to be clever. Nothing is to draw attention to the learning, the wisdom, the sophistication, the beauty, the complexity of the medium. Simple readings (not melodramatic), plain-style preaching, unadorned praying, and hearty singing are the need of the day. Frankly, this makes everything about worship leadership and participation more difficult. The leaders cannot fall back on processionals, incense, liturgy, ceremony, and ritual, or light-show, drama, dance, band, and multimedia presentation. The participants cannot sit back and enjoy the "show" as an audience before whom these liturgists or techies perform. Men with depth of character and godliness are the only vessels through which spiritual and simple worship will flow. Open minds and hearts are the only kind in which it will be received.

Third, worship that is "in spirit" is reverent. The spirit of worship is the spirit of reverence. The saints are to "offer to God an acceptable service with *reverence and awe*" (Heb 12:28). Worship is never conducted with a light or frivolous touch. When we pray, we pray not merely "Our Father," but "Our Father who art in *heaven, hallowed* be Thy name." Our concern in prayer and all our worship is that God's name be honored and revered, or *hallowed*, because He is the Father *in heaven*. True worship must always be serious, substantial, solid, sober, reverent.

What is reverence? The Bible doesn't leave us to pour into that word whatever content we wish. Reverence is righteous *fear*. Missing from the whole discussion of worship today is an appreciation of the Biblical concept of the "fear of God." Such is unmistakably central to Old Testament spirituality. "It is the decisive religious factor in Old Testament piety," says one theological dictionary.[48] In the Old Testament "true religion is often regarded as synonymous with the fear of God," says another.[49] The fear (Heb. *yare*) of the Lord is the first sign of true belief (Exod 14:31), and it is the beginning of wisdom (Heb. *yirah*; Prov 1:7; Ps 111:10). The Lord's eye is upon those that fear Him (Ps 33:18); He encamps about them and they suffer no want (Ps 34:7,9); His mercy is great toward them (Ps 103:11); He pities them (Ps 103:13); He blesses them (Ps 128:1); He fulfills their desire (Ps 145:19); and He takes pleasure in them (Ps 147:11). While this fear is not terror, neither is it bland appreciation. There is a fear that is "due" to God (Ps 90:11). Consequently, those who fear God with righteous fear are also said to "tremble." Those who are approved of God are those who are "humble and

---

[48] Colin Brown (ed.), *The New International Dictionary of New Testament Theology*, Vol. 1 (Grand Rapids: Zondervan Publishing House, 1975), 622.

[49] J.D. Douglas (ed.), *The New Bible Dictionary* (Leicester, England: Inter-Varsity Press, 1962), 365.

contrite of spirit, and who *tremble* at (His) word" (Isa 66:2). "Hear the word of the Lord, you who tremble at His word" (Isa 66:5). In Ps 96:9, "Worship the Lord in holy attire" parallels "Tremble before Him, all the earth." Worshiping and trembling go hand in hand. All the earth is called to tremble before our God (Ps 77:18; 99:1; 104:32; Isa 64:2; Jer 33:9). Even our rejoicing is with trembling.

> Worship the Lord with reverence, and rejoice with trembling. (Ps 2:11).

Other physical expressions of reverence are described as well. These too help us to understand its meaning. The Psalmist says,

> At Thy holy temple I will bow in reverence for Thee. (Ps 5:7b)

Because the Psalmist reverences (Heb. *yirah*) God, he bows. Again, the Psalmist says,

> Come, let us worship and bow down; Let us kneel before the Lord our Maker. (Ps 95:6)

Bowing and kneeling are appropriate responses for one who is in the presence of God (Ps 138:2). Moses "made haste to bow low to the earth and worship," when God passed before him (Exod 34:8). Solomon knelt as he prayed (2 Chr 6:3), and the whole people "bowed down" as they "worshiped and gave praise to the Lord" (2 Chr 7:3). Similarly, Ezra fell on his knees in confession, lay prostrate, and later the whole people "bowed low and worshiped the Lord with their faces to the ground" (Ezra 9:5,6; 10:1; Neh 8:6).

When we move into the New Testament is there any significant change? No, the piety of the Old Testament, the piety of the Psalms, of the Prophets, and of Proverbs, is the piety of the New Testament, only more so. Jesus assumed this continuity in saying,

> And do not fear those who kill the body, but are unable to kill the soul; but rather fear Him who is able to destroy both soul and body in hell. (Matt 10:28)

While this is not terror, it is a strong fear (Gk. *phobos*) that Jesus commended. He also assumed this continuity in His parable of the persistent widow, who approached a judge who "did not fear God and did not respect man" (Luke 18:1,2,4). The New Testament defines the ungodly as those who do not fear God (Rom 3:18), whereas Christians are those who are "walking in the fear of the Lord" (Acts 9:31). The fear of God is regularly appealed to as a motivation for Christian living. Christians are "perfecting holiness in the fear of God" (2 Cor 7:1), "subject to one another in the fear of God" (Eph 5:21), and they "conduct (them)selves with fear during the time of (their) stay upon earth." This last reference bears examination:

> And if you address as Father the One who impartially judges according to each man's work, conduct yourselves in fear during the time of your stay upon earth; (1 Pet 1:17)

Here the themes of sonship and fear are brought together. If the judge is our Father, we are to conduct ourselves with fear! (cf. Rom 11:20; Col 3:22; Heb 4:1; 1 Pet 2:17). According to the final book of the Bible, heaven is populated by those who fear God (Rev 11:18). Both the calls to the gospel and the calls to worship found in the Revelation are calls to fear God (Rev 14:7; 15:4; 19:5).

Neither is fear in the New Testament without trembling, prostration, and bowing. The Apostle Paul says,

> So then, my beloved, just as you have always obeyed, not as in my presence only, but now much more in my absence, work out your salvation with fear and trembling; (Phil 2:12)

"Fear and trembling" are joined here and elsewhere in the New Testament as they are in the Old Testament. The Corinthians are commended because their obedience was accompanied by "fear and trembling" (2 Cor 7:15; cf. 1 Cor 2:3; Eph 6:5). Similarly the Apostle John, when given a vision of Christ upon His throne, "fell at His feet as a dead man" (Rev 1:17). Paul concludes the extended prayer that began his epistle to the Ephesians, saying

> For this reason, I bow my knees before the Father (Eph 3:14)

He also promises that one day,

> *that at the name of Jesus every knee should bow, of those*
> *who are in heaven, and on earth, and under the earth,*
> *and that every tongue should confess that Jesus Christ is*
> *Lord, to the glory of God the Father.* (Phil 2:10, 11)

Finally, we read of the 24 elders of Revelation that they "fell down before Him who sits on the Throne," that they "fell down and worshiped" (Rev 4:10; 5:14; cf. 5:8). Old Testament and New Testament reverence is a godly fear, such as might be expressed through trembling, kneeling, bowing, and prostration.

If God is not concerned about posture, He certainly is concerned about the heart attitudes which reflect such bodily movements. Some authors want to avoid words like "serious" and "solemn," and advocate a friendly, light, informal atmosphere for worship. But one wonders how it could possibly be done and still remain true to the Biblical concept of reverence.[50] How else does one describe the mood of the assembly where the worshipers might be trembling, or kneeling, or bowing, or prostrate before the Almighty?

What about joy? That depends on what one means by joy. Christian joy is not the joy of the barroom or the ballfield, but of those who fear the God whom they love. Again it may be helpful to make some distinctions. Even in the athletic world there is a difference between the joy expressed when the winning touchdown is scored and that expressed at the awards banquet two months later. In both cases the emotion is joy, yet the manner of expressing it differs as one moves from one setting to another. Similarly the joy of worship is not like the arena. Such joy is not

---

[50] Frame finds "no scriptural reason" to believe that worship services should be conducted in a "solemn atmosphere." He reduces "dignity" to "a code word for formality," and claims that "the New Testament nowhere commands formality in worship." "All in all" he says, "it seems to me that the relevant considerations favor an informal service with a friendly, welcoming atmosphere and contemporary styles in language and music" (*Worship*, 82, 84).

expressed by high-fives, by jumping up and down, by screams and shouts. I once heard a preacher ask why we don't get as excited in church as we do at the football stadium. The answer is, that kind of excitement is unsuitable for public worship, and it is a different kind of joy. "Delight" and "fear" stand side by side in Psalm 112:1. As we've just noted, Christian joy is compatible with "trembling" (Ps 2:11). Presumably the 24 elders were filled with joy even as they fell prostrate before God. Indeed prostration and joy are joined in the experience of the wise men, who "rejoiced exceedingly with great joy . . . and fell down and worshiped Him" (Matt 2:10, 11). Our joy is a deep emotion, similar to peace, experienced at a level unrecognized by the world. It is not the noisy excitement of the arena, but is "inexpressible and full of glory" (1 Pet 1:8). John Newton put it this way:

> Savior, if of Zion's city
> I, through grace, a member am,
> Let the world deride or pity,
> I will glory in thy name:
> Fading is the worldling's pleasure,
> All his boasted pomp and show;
> Solid joys and lasting treasure
> None but Zion's children know.

"Pomp and show" is the "worldling's pleasure." It fades quickly. The world knows only the fleeting pleasure of temporary excitement. It is experienced in a moment and then vanishes. Our joys are the "solid joys" that only "Zion's children" experience. Bard Thompson in *Liturgies of the Western Church* explains of Calvin's liturgy that it "was directed *Soli Deo Gloria*, though in the same subdued and austere fashion that shaped all of Calvinist piety."[51] Our joy is a reverential joy, and in public displayed with restraint. Ostentatious displays of zeal, whether by shouting, by raising hands, by leaping about, or by other

---

[51] Bard Thompson, *Liturgies of the Western Church* (Philadelphia: Fortress Press, 1961), 193.

physical manifestations, have been restrained in Reformed circles by a sense of what is appropriate in a public worship service, as well as the desire not to draw attention to oneself or to claim too much for oneself. We do not pray so as to be seen by man, whether on the street corner or in the sanctuary. God alone is to be glorified (Matt 6:1-18).

Wise

Fourth, worship that is "in spirit" is wisely concluded. In the PCA (my denomination) we regrettably are split between *pragmatists*, who are ready to jettison all the distincitves of Reformed worship for the sake of "success" in ministry, and the *purists*, who are attempting to lift Reformed worship out of the 17th century, undiluted and unaltered, and reintroduce it into the 21st. What is needed is a new breed of "pragmatic purists," wise and sensible leaders who will champion Reformed worship but who will go about reforming today's worship wisely. We need "wise master builder(s)" who will repudiate the quick-building expedients of "wood, hay, stubble," and build only out of the Word-rich elements of "gold, silver, precious stones" (1 Cor 3:10-15). But as "wise master-builders" they will proceed with caution, sensitivity, and discernment.

Foolishness is manifest on both sides of the worship issue, by those who follow the contemporary trends reducing the Biblical content of public services (with less Bible read, preached, sung, and prayed), and by those who, in the name of Reformed worship, have reinstituted its distinctives too quickly and in indigestible quantities. The congregations of the former are starving on a milk-only diet, while those of the latter are choking on indigestible red meat. Reform your worship. But do so wisely.

When you *lead worship*, get the right tone and pace. Don't rush. Don't crawl. Be reverent, not frivolous, joyous, not miserable.

When you *preach*, expound a text, don't just give a talk; illustrate it, but don't let the whole sermon become storytelling; and aim at 30 minutes, not 15 ("sermonettes breed

Christianettes," says John Stott), and not 45 to 60 minutes. Why not? Because it is *unwise* to preach sermons that are too short *or* too long.

When you *pray* (thinking here of the traditional pastoral prayer), don't cheapen the value of prayer by reducing it to two minutes, but don't try the patience of your people by praying for 7 to 10 minutes either.

When you *sing*, don't sing silly camp-fire or revival-meeting songs, but don't overwhelm your people with heavy psalms and hymns all at once either. Proceed with discernment and wisdom.[52]

---

[52] For more on wise leadership in worship, see *Leading in Worship*, 15-18, 67-70, 103-104; *The Pastor's Public Ministry*, 1- 76.

4. Concluding Issues

PERHAPS IT IS NOW NECESSARY TO DISCUSS FURTHER THE "subdued and austere" nature of Reformed piety in light of the claims that are made regarding these physical expressions of exuberance. Dancing (Pss 149 and 150), shouting, clapping (Ps 47), and raising hands (numerous texts) are all pointed to as Biblical expressions of praise that ought to be used in the church. One proponent even thinks it "preposterous"[53] that we should think that Scripture and its regulative principle should forbid dance in worship. Leaving aside the not inconsiderable fact that no one, but no one, within Christendom's orthodox stream, whether Greek Orthodox, Roman Catholic, or Protestant, has advocated or defended dance as a part of Christian worship until recent times, other observations are in order about the way in which the Psalms and other texts are being used to advance worship that is physically demonstrative.

First, the Psalms from which most of the examples are drawn describe personal *emotions* and *actions* which are not necessarily intended to be acted out in public worship. Let me cite some examples. Over one-third of the Psalms may be classified as songs of lament or complaint. The Psalmist describes himself as groaning, crying, sighing, tearful, grieved, confused, lonely, afflicted, mourning, bent over and greatly bowed down, benumbed, crushed, anxious, sorrowful, despairing, sick, killed and slaughtered (Pss 5:1, 2; 6:6-7; 10; 25:16, 18; 38:6-9, 15-17; 42:1ff; 69:20; 44:22; etc.). Are we to believe that because these emotions and actions are found in the Psalms that they should be expressed in public worship? Are we to believe that when the Psalms are sung or read in worship that they constitute a call to audible groans, cries, and sighs? Must the worshipers adopt the emotions therein described? The mental attitude? The bodily

---

[53] Frame, *Worship*, 131. This seems to us a less-than-humble way to refer to the views of one's theological opponents.

posture? Must we sing descriptions of sighs and tears through our sighs and tears? A highly selective reading of the Psalms is required of those who call for physical or audible demonstrations of hand-raising, clapping, dancing, and shouting, and yet do not also call for prostration, crying and groaning. In worship there is much that we recall in which at that moment we are not meant to engage.

Second, the Psalms recall *events* from the life of Israel in which praise was expressed in forms not typical of the public assembly. For example, Ps 47 recalls the movement of the ark of the covenant from the house of Obed-edom to Jerusalem. That movement had the character of a parade, of a victory celebration with trumpets, shouting, and dancing (2 Sam 6:12-15). David himself, we are told, "was dancing before the Lord with all his might." But it is a far different thing to argue that the same expressions of joy would have been employed as the nation assembled before the holy of holies, or ought to be employed in the public assembly today. Dance may praise God if we think of worship in the "broad" sense. Weddings and other feasts and celebrations may have provided the occasions. For example, Miriam and the women of Israel celebrated with timbrels and dancing after the Red Sea closed over the Egyptian army, destroying it (Exod 5:20). But this was a public celebration, not a worship service. Ps 81 mentions public celebrations such as new moon, full moon, and feast days, and the exuberance shown on such days. We see again how vital it is that we distinguish things that differ. The Bible does not teach or suggest that dance is an approved and blessed element of public worship, and history knows no record of it being regarded as such in either the histories of Israel's temples and synagogues, or the Christian church. We can find no command, no example, and no promise.

The one New Testament reference to dance is found in 1 Corinthians 10:7. There Paul cites Exod 32:6 and the incident of the "golden calf."

> *And do not be idolaters, as some of them were; as it is written, "The people sat down to eat and drink, and stood up to play." (1 Cor 10:7)*

The "play" to which the text refers is described in Exod 32:19:
> And it came about, as soon as Moses came near the camp, that he saw the calf and the dancing; and Moses' anger burned, and he threw the tablets from his hands and shattered them at the foot of the mountain. (Exod 32:19)

The people were "dancing." Indeed, the RSV translates the Greek term (*paizein*, found only here in the New Testament) "to dance." While it has a range of meaning from "play, sport, jest . . . by joking, singing, and dancing" (so *Thayer*), or to "play, amuse oneself, dance" (so *Arndt & Gingrich*) its reference here is clearly to liturgical dance. Note: the Apostle Paul calls the participants "idolaters." The "dancing" around the golden calf is seen by Paul (and Moses!) as pagan idolatry, pure and simple. Such "play" was false worship, as much idolatrous as was the idol itself.

Dance is listed as an expression of praise in Psalms 149 and 150, yet those who appeal here to justify dance in worship must, once again, read their texts selectively. The same Psalm which says, "praise His name with dancing" also says,
> Let the godly ones exult in glory; Let them sing for joy on their beds. Let the high praises of God be in their mouth, and a two-edged sword in their hand. (Ps 149:5, 6)

Since the Psalm directs us to "sing for joy on (our) beds," shall we bring our cots into public worship? Since those with "the high praises of God" in their mouths also have a "two-edged sword in their hand," shall we bring our swords with us to services and flash them about as acts of worship? Surely it is clear that we cannot simplistically locate movements and actions in the Psalms, and argue on that basis alone that such necessarily belong in public worship. Because the Psalms recall events from the history of Israel, they describe public celebrations which involve elements (e.g. dances, the flashing of swords, shouts, the clapping of hands, etc.) which ordinarily may not be suitable for regular public worship.

Third, some practices being advocated today involve not just a selective reading, but a *misreading of their meaning in Scripture*.

We have particularly in mind the raising of one's hands. It is not difficult to determine the meaning of hand raising in Scripture. It is simply a posture for prayer. One may pray standing (the usual posture – 1 Sam 1:26; Matt 11:25; Luke 18:11,13), kneeling (2 Chr 6:13; Ps 95:6; Dan 6:10; Luke 22:41; Acts 7:60, 9:40, 20:36, 21:5), sitting (2 Sam 7:18), or prostrate (Num 16:22; Josh 5:14; Dan 8:17; Rev 1:17, 4:10, 5:8, 5:14, 11:16). The raising of one's hands is an acceptable part of one's posture for prayer. Moses' famous prayer during Israel's battle with Amalek provides a good example, but there are many others as well (Exod 17:9ff; Pss 28:1, 2, 63:4, 77:2, 119:47, 134:2, 141:2, 143:4, etc.). So then, if hands are to be raised in worship it should be done either symbolically on behalf of the congregation by the minister, or by the whole congregation itself throughout the prayer as a posture for intercession.

But the charismatic movement has taken what was a posture for prayer and turned it into a personal response to the excitement of the moment. When one is particularly moved by the events of the service one raises one's hands. That may or may not be an appropriate thing to do, but our point is that it is not a Biblical thing to do. One may not simply look in the Bible and find references to the lifting of the hands and then identify it with the practices of the group to which one belongs. Raised hands represent the lifting up of prayer to God, and so are an appropriate posture to assume when praying. The only thing that Biblical hand-raising has in common with Charismatic-type hand-raising is that the hands are up in the air. One is the posture of intercession. The other is a very ostentatious display of spiritual excitement, one which, in our view, is better not indulged.

* * *

So where does this leave us? A. W. Tozer wrote a pamphlet a few years ago entitled *Worship: The Missing Jewel of the Evangelical Church.* He lamented the irreverence of most of what passes for worship in conservative churches these days. Some continue to employ the revivalism model. Like the churches I grew up in, "worship" consists of light singing, light chatter, virtually no prayer, no confession of sin, little Bible reading, an evangelistic sermon, an altar call, and good-bye. It's really not a worship service – it's a "revival" meeting. Some have taken this same format and jazzed it up, adding choir productions and solos, and even drama, skits and dancing. I say it's a variation of the same theme because the audience is in the congregation, not in heaven. Whatever might be said to the contrary, the true intent is to perform for the people (including unbelievers in the crowd), not for the Lord. Isn't this why clapping has become commonplace at these services? Isn't this why our churches look more like theaters than churches?

The Charismatic alternative is little better, if at all. It encourages one to seek the Lord and delight in him, so that there exists a living dynamic absent in the more staid conservative churches. But the Charismatic style may fairly be described as non-cognitive. The praises and consequent thoughts of God are regularly trite, repetitious, and devoid of serious content. What the worshiper "feels" and experiences will tend to be superficial and self-centered. He is moved not by truth, but by what he feels, experience becoming an end in itself. This too, in the long run, will result in spiritual bankruptcy. One can dip into the emotional well only so many times. Wonderful while it lasts, eventually it comes up dry.

Many young people who have been brought up in these churches are voting with their feet and joining liturgical churches. Colleen Carroll's recent book, *The New Faithful*,[54] documents the movement to religious orthodoxy among substantial numbers of the young. Some are "On the Canterbury Trail," as Robert Weber put it. Others have joined Roman Catholic churches, and some have even followed the lead of a group of ex-Campus Crusaders

---

[54] Carroll, Colleen. *The New Faithful: Why Young Adults Are Embracing Christian Orthodoxy*, Chicago: Loyola Press, 2002; see also Oden, Thomas C. *The Rebirth of Orthodoxy*, Harper Collins Publishers, 2002.

and joined the Greek Orthodox church, which now has an "Evangelical Diocese" designed to accommodate evangelicals who wish to make the transition to Orthodoxy. Granted, worship as evangelism, therapy, or entertainment is bankrupt. It will not feed the soul. But neither will the alternative of ritual. The "smells and bells" of high-church ceremonies will not generate deep faith and will ultimately inhibit a deep personal knowledge of Christ. In one respect, it is just another form of entertainment, of pleasing the senses. It is more "religious" in form, but just as doubtful in effects.

What is the answer? The simple, spiritual, reverent worship of the Calvinistic heritage; worship in which we *read*, *preach*, *pray*, and *sing* the Bible. It alone can sustain and nurture Reformed faith and piety. Here we have order without suffocation, freedom without chaos, edification without entertainment, reverence without rote. Reformed worship aims *Soli Deo Gloria*, and in so doing provides a format in which true worship may take place. God is the focus and not man. God's word determines the order of worship and not the inventions and traditions of man. The glory then goes to God alone!

5. Recommended for Further Reading and Listening

Worship and Sacraments

Baird, Charles. *Presbyterian Liturgies*, Grand Rapids: Baker House, [1855], 1957.

Carson, D.A., ed., *Worship: Adoration and Action*, Eugene, Oregon: Wipf and Stock, 2002.

Carson, D.A., *Worship By the Book*, Grand Rapids, MI: Zondervan, 2002.

Carson, D.A., *A Call to Spiritual Reformation*, Grand Rapids, MI: Baker Academic, 1992.

Davies, Horton, *The Worship of the American Puritans*, Morgan, PA: Soli Deo Gloria Publications, [1990], 1999.

Davies, Horton, *The Worship of the English Puritans*, Morgan, PA: Soli Deo Gloria Publications, [1948], 1997.

Duncan, J. Ligon, III., *Worshipping God Together: Congregational Worship at First Presbyterian Church*, Jackson, MS: First Presbyterian Church, 2005.

Gordon, T. David. "Some Answers About the Regulative Principle," *Westminster Theological Journal*, 55, 1993, 321-29.

Hart, D.G., *Recovering Mother Kirk*, Grand Rapids: Baker Academic, 2003.

Hart, D.G. and J. Muether, *With Reverence and Awe*, Phillipsburg: Presbyterian and Reformed Publications, 2002

Johnson, Terry L. *Leading in Worship*, Oak Ridge, Tennessee: The Covenant Foundation, 1996.

Johnson, Terry L. *The Pastor's Public Ministry*, Greenville, South Carolina: Reformed Academic Press, 2001.

Nichols, James Hastings. *Corporate Worship in the Reformed Tradition*, Philadelphia: Westminster Press, 1968.

Old, Hughes Oliphant. *The Shaping of the Reformed Baptismal Rite in the Sixteenth Century*, Grand Rapids: Eerdmans, 1992.

Old, Hughes Oliphant. *Themes and Variations for a Christian Doxology*, Grand Rapids: Eerdmans, 1992.

Old, Hughes Oliphant. *Worship That Is Reformed According to Scriptures (Guides to the Reformed Tradition)*, Atlanta: John Knox Press, 1984.

Old, Hughes Oliphant. *The Patristic Roots of Reformed Worship*, Zurich: Theologischer Verlag, 1970.

Packer, J.I. "The Puritan Approach to Worship," in *A Quest for Godliness: The Puritan Vision of the Christian Life*, Wheaton: Crossway Books, 1990.

Rayburn, Robert. *O Come Let Us Worship*, Grand Rapids: Baker House Books, 1980.

Ryken, Phil, Derek Thomas, and J. Ligon Duncan, III, eds., Give Praise to God: A Vision for Reforming Worship, Phillipsburg, N.J.: P&R, 2003.

Thompson, Bard. *Liturgies of the Western Church*, Philadelphia: Fortress Press, 1961.

Preaching

Adams, Jay. *Preaching with Purpose*, Phillipsburg, New Jersey: Presbyterian and Reformed Publishing Company, 1982.

Alexander, J. W. *Thoughts on Preaching*, Edinburgh: The Banner of Truth, [1864], 1989.

Bridges, Charles. *The Christian Ministry*, Edinburgh: The Banner of Truth, [1854], 1958 (oup).

Dabney, R. L. *Sacred Rhetoric: or A Course of Lectures on Preaching*, Edinburgh: The Banner of Truth, [1870], 1979.

Davis, Ralph, *The Word Became Fresh*, Fearn, Rosshire: Christian Focus Publications, 2006.

Dever, Mark, et al, *Preaching the Cross* ,Wheaton, IL: Crossway, 2007.

Lloyd-Jones, D. Martin. *Preaching and Preachers*, Grand Rapids, Michigan: Zondervan, 1971.

Olds, Hughes Oliphant. *The Reading and Preaching of the Scriptures in the Worship of the Christian Church*, Volumes 1-4 (7 volumes projected), Grand Rapids: Eerdmans, 1998.

Perkins, William. *The Art of Prophesying*, Edinburgh: The Banner of Truth, [1606], 1996.

Shedd, W. G. T. *Homiletics and Pastoral Theology*, Edinburgh: The Banner of Truth, [1867], 1965.

Spurgeon, C. H. S. *Lectures to My Students*, Fearn, Rosshire: Christian Focus Publications, [1881-1894], 2000.

Still, William. *The Work of the Pastor*, Aberdeen: Didasko Press, 1976.

Public Prayer

Bennet, Arthur, ed., *The Valley of Vision: A Collection of Puritan Prayers & Devotions*, Edinburgh, Scotland: Banner of Truth, 2003 reprint.

Duncan, III, J. Ligon. (ed.), Matthew Henry's *A Method for Prayer*, Greenville: Reformed Academic Press, [1710], 1994.

Miller, Samuel. *Thoughts on Public Prayer*, Harrisonburg, Virginia: Sprinkle Publications, [1844], 1985.

Old, Hughes Oliphant. *Leading in Prayer*, Grand Rapids: Eerdmans, 1995.

Watts, Isaac. *A Guide to Prayer*, Edinburgh: The Banner of Truth Trust, [1715], 2001

Psalmody/Hymnody

Christian Hymns, Evangelical Movement of Wales, 1977.

Hymns Triumphant Vols. 1 and 2 (CD), Sparrow Records: 1981, 1984.

Psalms of the Trinity Psalter, Vols. I and II (CD), IPC Press, 1999, 2002.